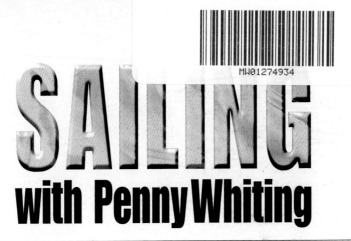

SAILING
with Penny Whiting

A step-by-step guide to the basics of sailing

REED

Established in 1907, Reed Publishing (NZ) Ltd
is New Zealand's largest book publisher, with over 300 titles in print.

For details on all these books visit our website:
www.reed.co.nz

Published by Reed Books, a division of Reed Publishing (NZ) Ltd, 39 Rawene Rd,
Birkenhead, Auckland 10. Associated companies, branches and representatives
throughout the world.

ISBN 0 7900 0818 1
First published 1984 as *The Penny Whiting Sailing Book* by Reed Methuen Ltd (Auckland)
Reprinted 1986
Revised edition published 1996 by Penguin Books (NZ) Ltd
Second revised edition published 2002 by Reed Publishing (NZ) Ltd

Printed in New Zealand

For Paul

contents

acknowledgements

It is my wish to acknowledge a few very prominent people in my sailing life. My parents Mollie and D'Arcy Whiting have always been great supporters of my ideas and have encouraged me during my long sailing career. D'Arcy and I have sailed many a mile aboard *Coruba* and *Tequila* with a family crew, often made up of Tony, Debbie and Grant Whiting. Their continued support and participation in my life will always be important to me.

During my early years of sailing at the Point Chevalier Sailing Club in Auckland, I learnt a lot and the club played a role in keeping me in line with my sailing antics in my OK dinghy yacht, *Tuppence*.

In my late teens I sailed thousands of miles aboard *Kahurangi* with L.D. Nathan and friends and these years were very significant to my sailing career. *Kahurangi* was a special yacht and was always kept in immaculate condition.

Working for Chris Bouzaid in my early years and sailing with him and his wife, Trice, from place to place has always been fun.

Serious competition was part of my sailing career, with my brother Paul Whiting and Alan Warwick aboard the fantastic little keeler called *Reactor*.

I wish to acknowledge Doc Williams for his assistance in writing the rules of boating with me.

In recent years I have so enjoyed the thrill of sailing aboard the 65-foot *Antaeus*, Charles and Rosemary Brown's ocean racer.

To my children, Carl and Erin — we sure have sailed some miles around the Northland coast in *Avian*, *Northerner* and *Endless Summer*. You both steered a great course and never gave up when the tough got tougher out on the coast — you are both great crew and I love sailing with you.

Several others have been significant in my sailing life, far too many to put on this page, but you know who you are, so thank you for your friendship and support.

Penny Whiting, MBE

introduction

IN NEW ZEALAND we are very much connected with the sea. There is not one great yachting event in the world that happens without a Kiwi in there somewhere making a significant contribution. New Zealand yachtsmen and women have a unique reputation and are always in demand as designers, skippers, sailmakers and crew, with their ultimate yacht-racing success the America's Cup.

They are carrying on traditions that go back to the last century. Eighty to ninety years ago the Logans and the Baileys were building fine yachts from heart kauri — many of these beautiful craft are still sailing today — and from these beginnings have come today's innovative designers and builders of world-class boats, and the skippers and crew who sail them.

The sport has always been open to everyone in this country. There is no privileged class in New Zealand yachting — if you have a desire to mess about in boats, you can. It may only be in a 10-footer — but you are the skipper, the helm is yours.

My father D'arcy, an old salt, made one of his early voyages as a small boy in a corrugated iron dinghy. His voyage took him from Herne Bay to Watchman's Island using his parents' double sheet as a sail. I spent many happy hours as a small girl exploring the bays in and around Auckland in my OK dinghy. Lovely nights were spent under the stars, tucked up in my sleeping bag. *Tuppence* was a fine little ship and carried me safely wherever I wanted to go. I once made a memorable voyage from Sandspit to Kawau Island. I capsized three times, drenched my sleeping bag and lost Mum's bacon and egg pie. What an adventure! How proud I was on reaching port. Since then I have travelled over 30,000 sea miles.

The Hauraki Gulf is my great love. I have been to some wonderful and exciting places around the world but I feel that nothing can match the waters here. The Hauraki Gulf must be the finest cruising ground in the world; but a cheer for those who get their enjoyment from tackling the waters of Wellington or Lyttelton and all the other bays and harbours along the coast; and to those who venture inland looking for their fun on the lovely freshwater lakes of both islands. Sailing is a wonderful pastime with endless opportunities for everyone.

'If it's hard to do, then you're doing it the wrong way. The easy way is the right way'.

It has given me great pleasure to be able to introduce people of all ages to the joy and excitement of sailing. I have been teaching since 1968, first using my father's sloop *Coruba* in Auckland, then later on the beautiful waters of Vancouver Harbour, Canada, aboard the former America's Cup challenger *Dame Pattie*. D'arcy sold *Coruba* and built *Tequila*. Designed by my brother Paul, *Tequila* became my schoolboat in Auckland and then in Miami during my parents' passage around America. Back in Auckland I bought *Avian* and taught on her for six years. In 1981 I purchased *Northerner*, the 15-metre Stewart sloop, which had such a proud racing record before it came into my life. Four years later I replaced her with a Whiting 47, designed by my brother Paul, and named *Endless Summer*.

I have taught thousands of people to sail, including hundreds of children, and I do wish to emphasise that sailing is not a sport or pastime that requires brute strength. The heaviest thing you will ever have to do is to get the sail out of the cabin, through the hatch and onto the deck; or to lower or pull up the anchor or to get your trailer

The basics of sailing apply to any boat you may wish to sail, from keelers to trailer sailers and small centreboard yachts. If you have the chance, learning the rudiments aboard a keeler will make it all a lot easier, and give you greater confidence. But if learning on a small boat, the principles and terms will be the same, and nearly everything in this book is applicable to any boat.

sailer on and off its trailer. But for actual sailing, sheer brute strength just doesn't come into it. It's all about timing. The correct way is the easiest.

If anything else is proving hard to do, then you're simply doing it the wrong way — sailing is easy! It's simply knowing how to, and doing things the right way.

In the children's classes, the kids are usually between five and twelve and at those ages they learn fast. I believe that you must teach children to sail a large yacht because what breaks up many family yachting trips is the children not being allowed to participate in the sailing. So they get bored and would rather go tramping or do anything else than sit on a boat where they cannot contribute. If you can keep your family involved and sailing, it will help you keep the boat a lot longer.

I have always felt that a keeler is the ideal type of yacht to learn on. Even if the beginner ultimately buys a sailing dinghy, I'm sure he or she will pick up sailing skills more quickly on a keeler because the size and stability of a big boat helps build early confidence. Further, learning in a class provides opportunities to observe others and learn from mistakes. Once the basics are understood and have been tested in a practical way, you have the knowledge to sail any type of yacht.

Of course, it isn't always possible to have your first taste of sailing aboard a keeler and this book has been written so that novices on board any kind of sailing craft can adapt the information to suit. This book covers what I believe are the basics of sailing that must be understood by all beginners. Without this knowledge you are a liability, not only to yourself but also to the boat you sail on. The core of the book is a step-by-step guide that will enable you to go out there and sail, and build experience. For reading alone won't make you a sailor. If possible, try to sail with someone experienced with whom you can test your knowledge. Take any opportunity to sail on different kinds of yachts. Sail as much as you can.

Penny Whiting MBE
Auckland

a boat of your own

I EXPECT THAT if you have a real hankering to go sailing you will already have done a few sea miles of 'dream cruising', drifting off to some quiet bay where you relax as your yacht swings gently at anchor . . .

The good thing about this type of cruising is that it may be done any time. Many a fine cruise has been completed during an important meeting or on the daily ride home in the bus. I once heard of someone who had even circumnavigated the world during a rather tedious conference.

If you have a real desire to go yachting, I bet that not too many cruises later you will be spending a few hours strolling around marinas or browsing through yachting magazines. This is the second and most dangerous stage. You have become a waterfront sailor! Buying your first yacht will be a mixture of excitement, joy and fear. The day the transaction is completed you will be as nervous as if you were landing at Wellington Airport in a 40-knot southerly.

Let's look at the various alternatives that are open to you — considering first of all your personal requirements.

Do you want a day sailer, a racer, or a cruising boat?

Where will you keep it? Will your boat need a mooring or a marina, or are you going to buy a trailer sailer and tow it to and from the launching ramp?

Do you want a traditional wooden construction — on which there will be more annual maintenance — or do you want a low maintenance fibreglass craft?

What about experience . . . some boats can be sailed readily by a couple with young children; others need three to four experienced adults.

The larger the yacht you can afford (within reason), the easier it will be to handle.

Generally, however, there are three points the first-time boat owner should keep in mind; these are:

1   Buy a yacht that has a good resale value.
2   Use the services of a yacht broker.
3   Buy the best you can for the money you have available.

Resale value — although by the time it comes to buying your first boat you will have looked at hundreds of photos and read dozens of descriptions of the various types, talked to your friends and perused the boat ads, it's a good bet that in the first year of sailing your ideas of what you want out of a boat will change dramatically. In the second year or so of sailing their own boats, a lot of people decide to make a change. Understandably, this reflects the experience they have gained as a first-time sailor and yacht owner — which all means that your first boat should be one that will sell easily enough when your requirements change.

New or second-hand — new boats will have lower maintenance but they can bring with them some teething troubles for novice sailors. On the other hand, a second-hand yacht will have been used for various types of sailing and the previous owner or owners will probably have added extra gear and equipment. They will have done so because they found they needed it. So if you are a learner and someone else has sorted out the bugs in the boat, that's a few less headaches for you.

Whichever way you go, however, keep in mind that new or second-hand, your boat should be easy to resell.

A yachtbroker — brokers provide an excellent service and will be of help in all aspects of your purchase, including advising on finance. They will be able to show you a large variety of craft from trailer sailers up, and over a wide price range so you may better appreciate the trends of the market. And yachtbrokers do not charge you, the buyer, for their services; like land agents, they receive a fee from the vendor.

What you buy will obviously depend upon your budget but keep in mind that, like a lot of other purchases, it pays to go for quality. A boat that is well founded will repay you many times over in trouble-free sailing and the long life of its gear. A good-sized boat with quality gear will be easier to sell later on.

Survey — although not strictly necessary, a survey is strongly recommended, even though you must pay for it regardless of whether you buy the boat or not. A yachtbroker will help you with the names of local surveyors or you may be able to find one yourself through the Yellow Pages or in the classified ads of boating magazines.

The surveyor will arrange to have the yacht hauled out, checked over, and will provide you with a comprehensive report on its seaworthiness. As well, you should arrange for a sea trial on a windy day. If repairs are necessary, these may be estimated by a boatbuilder.

Large yachts are not cheap, and whether the boat is being sold through a broker or privately, it's advisable to have it surveyed. The surveyor's cost is small compared with the thousands of dollars that may be spent on a mistake.

Before you finalise your purchase, ask to see the inventory, the list of what goes with the yacht when it's sold to you. It saves problems and arguments later if you know beforehand that the single-side-band radio and depth sounder are not included in the purchase price and the owner will be taking them off the boat when the deal is completed. Also, if you are buying privately, don't forget to find out if there are any outstanding hire-purchase payments to be made on the vessel, or other debts. If the boat is New Zealand registered, an inspection of the registry at the particular port will reveal any encumbrances.

Selling — as with buying, you can either sell your yacht privately

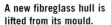

A new fibreglass hull is lifted from its mould.

or put it in the hands of a broker. In the case of the former, you are still able to obtain a valuation from the broker for a small fee, a valuation that will be of help in fixing your selling price. The advantage in having it with a broker is that he or she is able to give it more exposure to potential buyers than you can privately. As mentioned above, as the vendor you pay the broker's fee by way of a percentage of the selling price.

yacht types

No matter what you buy or build, your yacht will be classified by the rig it carries. Yacht types are easily identified by the rig they carry.

Sloop — the most functional and popularly used rig, on yachts from 10 to 80 feet (3 to 24 metres). A single mast with the forestay running to the mast-head. One mast and various changeable headsails.

Fractional rig — similar to a sloop but with the forestay running from a fraction of the way down the mast — about three-quarters of the way up. These yachts carry smaller headsails and larger mains than mast-head sloops and while they don't have to carry as many sail combinations, they do require skill to sail them well. Fractional rigs have been developed from racing sailing dinghies and today this rig is seen on many top racing yachts up to 60 feet (20 metres). It

Rig types

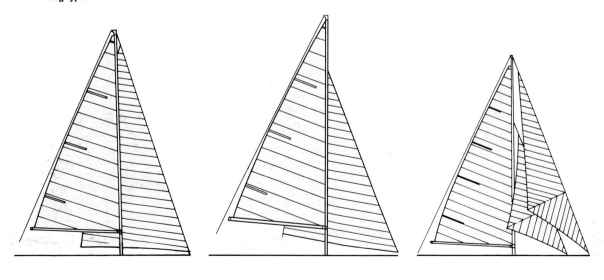

Sloop   Fractional   Cutter

is also the rig carried by many trailer sailers. However, a fractionally-rigged mast requires more tuning and care than a sloop-rigged one, because of running back stays and the bend in the top of the mast.

Cutter — not so popular today, the cutter rig features multiple headsail combinations carried on two forestays instead of the one used in sloops and fractional rigs. This set-up is great on big yachts.

Ketch — a two-masted format, the shorter mizzen mast aft stepped forward of the rudder post. The mizzen aids in steering, especially in heavy weather. A ketch has more sail combination than other yachts, but its advantages are somewhat outweighed by the simple fact that there is more to do.

Yawl — another two-masted yacht not in vogue today. It differs from the ketch only in the placement of the mizzen mast, which is closer to the stern and aft of the rudder post. The mizzen sail of a yawl is smaller than that of a ketch, but has the same function.

Schooner — yachting's most romantic rig. There are many different combinations according to the size of the yacht and the number of masts. In a two-master, the small foremast is stepped forward of the main.

Hull types also vary and, like rigs, are another factor for consideration when buying a yacht. If thinking of a keeler, for instance, you'll also need a mooring or marina berth, and these are usually in short supply. Try to arrange a mooring or berth before you

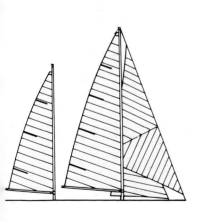

Ketch

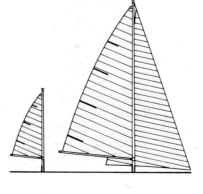

Yawl

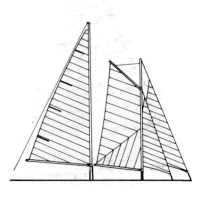

Schooner

buy your keeler, or look for a secondhand boat that is being sold with one. On the other hand, remember that a trailer sailer will involve more time and preparation for launching and recovery, and require a powerful towing vehicle. So a trailer sailer may not necessarily be cheaper.

Fin keel — the look of most modern designs, the size and shape of the fin depending on the yacht. Sailing efficiency of this type of keel has been improved greatly over the last 25 years, and fin keels can now be just as stable as the older long keels, and lighter to steer. The modern versions are long, with the weight low .

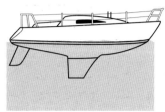

Fin keel

Winged keel — made famous by the Australian designer, the late Ben Lexan, who used it on Australia III when the Aussies won the America's Cup in 1983. It enables a boat in certain conditions to achieve better windward and tacking performance. Developments of the winged keel were seen at the 1986 America's Cup in Perth. It is sure to continue as an interesting design option and has been used on boats other than the 12-metre, where its advantages can be used to the full.

Long keel — the traditional underwater profile of the cruising yacht. The deep-drafted, long-keel shape dominated design thinking for many decades and is still popular with those who like the heavier displacement, older-style yacht. Such a boat keeps its course well but is heavy to turn and not as effective as the modern fin keel on all points of sailing. Requires a more powerful rig than a fin keel of the same length.

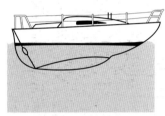

Long keel

Bilge keel — makes for a shallow-drafted yacht, with the two keels fitted on the turn of the bilge. A useful boat for shallow waterways. It can be moored close to a beach where the bottom is level and reasonably hard so at low tide the hull remains upright. Windward performance is not as good as a fin keel.

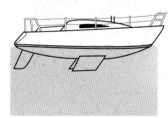

Bilge keel

Drop keel or centreboard — most common today on trailer sailers. The keel is raised and lowered by a winch to enable the yacht to be placed on a trailer. Draft is greatly reduced when the keel is raised. The rudder is also retractable.

Catamaran — two-hulled, light-displacement yacht. Popular as a fast cruising yacht that provides flat sailing. Needs to be sailed well: if capsized, a catamaran will stay upside-down.

Trimaran — a yacht with two outriggers off either side of a centre hull. Like the catamaran, a fast, light-displacement format. The centre hull usually incorporates a centreboard.

Trailer sailers — I feel a special note is due regarding trailer sailers. It concerns me that so many beginners — let alone families

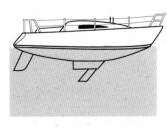

Drop keel (centreboard)

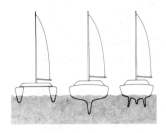

Front view of *(left to right)* **underwater profiles of catamaran, fin keel and bilge keel.**

— have leapt into trailer sailers for their first big-boat sailing experience, expecting them to be able to perform like a keeler. There is no doubt that trailer sailers are, in the main, well designed and built, but they do have limitations.

The major drawback is that, unlike keelers, most trailer sailers are unable to be righted if they capsize. You do two or three things wrong at the same time and they can go over and stay over. A keeler cannot capsize whereas a trailer sailer, catamaran or trimaran can, if things go wrong.

The newcomer to big-boat sailing should gain some keeler experience to appreciate the differences, and then sail his or her trailer sailer within limits.

The sloop rig is yachting's most popular rig, tried and proven as a dependable no-fuss rig.

know your boat — an ABC of structure, rigging and fittings

AT FIRST GLANCE the terminology of sailing can appear confusing. It seems as though the English language has been abandoned: words like 'front' and 'back' have been replaced by 'forward' and 'aft', 'ropes' become 'sheets' or 'halyards', and it's difficult to tell your leech from your luff. But the language of sailing is an old and traditional one and such terms must be learnt and the functions of the parts understood. From this fundamental knowledge will come an understanding of how the hull, rigging, fittings and sails work in with each other effectively to transform the force of the wind into forward motion through the water.

Rigging consists of standing rigging all the wires that hold up the boat's masts; and running rigging all the lines, halyards, and sheets used to raise and lower sails, and to pull them in and let them out.

The fittings comprise a system of winches, cleats and blocks.

The mast of today's yachts is usually alloy extrusion that allows halyards to be housed inside it. The track on the aft edge of the mast carries the slides of the mainsail's luff edge.

The stays, also known as shrouds or rigging, are wires that stay up, or support the mast. The forestay and backstay run from the top of the mast to the bow and stern respectively. Sidestays usually include both upper shrouds, which run from the top of the mast over spreaders to the side edges of the deck, and lower shrouds, which extend down from the base of the spreaders to the deck. The forestay and backstay support it across the centre of the yacht.

The spreaders are used to 'spread' the angle of the load the upper shrouds make with the top of the mast, and make for better support of the top section of the mast. But the spreaders also result in a force that tends to bend the mast at that point and the lower shrouds are attached — further down the mast beneath the spreaders — to counteract this bend. With stays and shrouds, tension is adjusted by means of turnbuckles or rigging screws. Once set, they need very little further adjustment.

The topping lift holds up the boom when the mainsail is not up, or when the mainsail is being reefed. The topping lift wire or rope is

An understanding of a boat's structure and gear, and how the various components work together, will enable the helmsman to sail efficiently and effectively. This yacht has a three-quarter rig.

Topping lift wire hangs loose when mainsail is hoisted.

Self-tailing jib sheet winch.

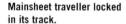

Mainsheet traveller locked in its track.

attached to the aft end of the boom and runs through the top of the mast down to a mast cleat.

The rudder is turned by either a tiller connecting directly to the rudderstock, or wheel connected to a steering box. Yachts under about 10 metres tend to have tillers and those over that length, wheels. On a large keeler, a tiller would have to be very long to gain the necessary leverage and would take up a lot of cockpit room: a wheel gives more control and is more compact.

The keel supplies transverse stability against the heeling action of the wind on the sails. As well it helps resist leeway. The keel can be a solid lead, concrete or metal fin attached below the frame, or take the form of ballast secured inside the hull.

Stanchions are upright metal posts attached to the deck and which support lifelines and rails around the edge of the deck. The guard rail at the bow is called the pulpit; and that at the stern, the pushpit.

The coaming is the raised edge around the cockpit and hatchway that helps to protect the crew from spray as well as forming a base for winches and cleats. The cabin sides are also coamings.

Winches are geared metal drums used to gain sheet or halyard tension when pulling sails in or up.

A fairlead is a fitting used to alter the direction of a rope passed through it. Fairleads are placed to lead sheets and halyards correctly onto winches, though less commonly these days.

Blocks and pulleys are also used to change the direction of pull on a sheet or halyard. The rope runs over a sheave in the block, which makes for minimum friction and an easier pull.

The boom vang, or kicking strap, is a line joining the underside of the boom to the base of the mast. It is used to pull the boom down and keep·it from kicking up when the sail is eased out and is full of wind. By pulling the boom vang in tight, the roll of the boat is controlled.

The mainsheet traveller is a fitting that runs on a track athwartships close to the cockpit or over the aft cabin top, and to which is attached mainsheet blocks. The mainsheet runs through the traveller block to the mainsheet block on the boom. The mainsheet traveller helps control the shape of the sail and the weight on the steering. By moving the traveller to leeward, wind can be spilled from the sail. If moved to windward, the sail is 'hooked' in more. Central sheeting of the traveller is wise most of the time except when you are racing and have enough crew to play with it.

The gooseneck is a fitting that attaches the boom to the mast.

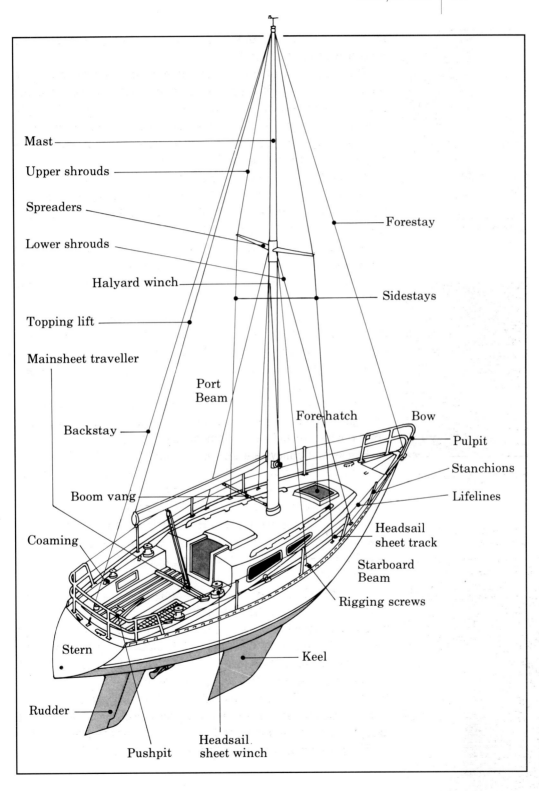

Mast

Upper shrouds

Spreaders

Lower shrouds

Halyard winch

Topping lift

Mainsheet traveller

Backstay

Boom vang

Coaming

Stern

Rudder

Port Beam

Fore hatch

Bow

Forestay

Sidestays

Pulpit

Stanchions

Lifelines

Headsail sheet track

Starboard Beam

Rigging screws

Keel

Pushpit

Headsail sheet winch

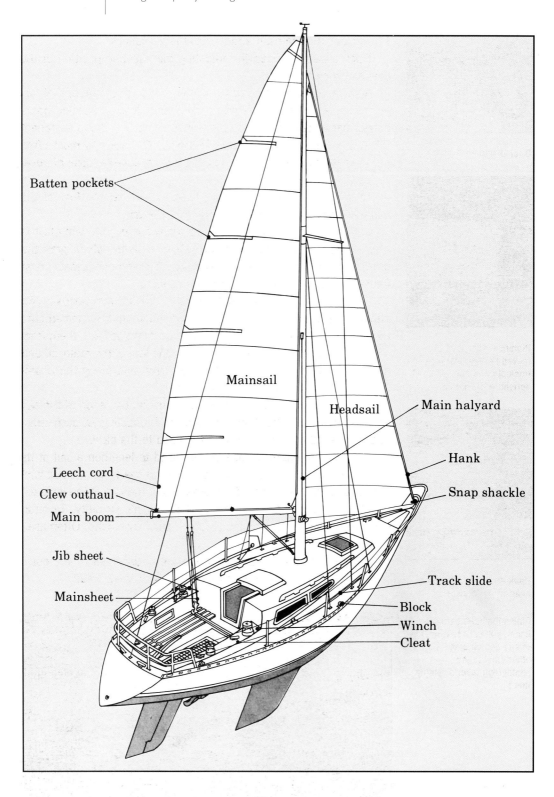

Batten pockets

Mainsail

Headsail

Main halyard

Hank

Leech cord

Clew outhaul

Main boom

Snap shackle

Jib sheet

Mainsheet

Track slide

Block

Winch

Cleat

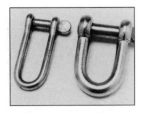

D- or U-shackle.

Picture shows jib sheet reeved through block on track slide. Block is lashed upright to the lifeline.

Hank used to attach luff of headsail to forestay.

Outhaul is pulled along boom, pulled to tension foot of sail and cleated. (The other cleat in the photograph is for a reefing line.)

The tack of the mainsail attaches to the gooseneck.

Track slides are used for adjusting the sheeting position of the headsail sheets.

A shackle is a metal fitting, usually of a D- or U-shape, that has a removable screw-pin across its open end. A snap shackle has a hinged bar instead of a loose pin across its open end and so cannot fall out and be lost overboard. This type of shackle is most often found at the bow where there is more risk of losing a loose pin over the side.

The outhaul is a rope or wire used to pull out the foot of the mainsail to control its foot tension along the boom.

Cleats are fittings to which ropes are secured. The cam cleat is a type of jamming cleat with spring-loaded teeth, which grab the rope. Both it and the jam cleat are quick-release cleats most frequently used on mainsheets and jib sheets.

Hanks are clips fastened onto the luff of the headsail for attaching it to the forestay. Vaseline or similar can be smeared onto the working parts of the hanks every few months to keep them free.

Slides are fastened to the luff and to the foot of the mainsail and are used to carry the sail up the mast track and along the boom. They are usually plastic or stainless steel.

The leechcord is a line running down inside the leech of the sail and with which the leech can be tightened, enabling an even curve to be achieved on the leech from the head to the clew.

A strop is a length of rope or wire used to lengthen a sail at its tack or head. A strop is often used between the tack of a headsail and its attachment at the bow in order to get the foot of the headsail up off the deck and so assist the helmsman's visibility. To strop down is to secure something so that it cannot fly around. Often used on the main halyard.

A sheet is a rope used to control a sail's movement in and out.

A halyard is a rope or wire used to hoist or lower a sail.

ropes, knots, rope-handling and splicing (suitable for any size of yacht)

AT FIRST, THE COCKPIT and deck of a yacht may seem to be littered with a confusing array of ropes and lines, but after a short time sailing you will achieve an understanding of how the running rigging operates, and be able to identify various sheets and halyards and understand their purpose more readily. You will be aided to some degree by rope manufacturers who have tried to simplify matters through producing braided ropes.

Synthetic braids have replaced the traditional natural fibre ropes of early sailing. Synthetic ropes are easier to handle as they do not stretch as much, if at all, and also have the advantage of resistance to sun, rot, stretch and wear.

Every boat should carry a sail repair kit that contains tools for working with rope.

knots

There have been whole books written and illustrated on how to do thousands of knots, and of all those only four are worth remembering. These are the reef knot, bowline, clove hitch, and figure-8 knot. If you know how to do these in daylight and in

Sail tie securing furled sail is knotted with a reef knot. A tail slipped into the end of the knot allows it to be more easily undone.

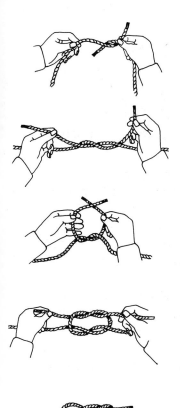

darkness you will be able to cope with most situations on board a boat. As well, of course, they are extremely useful elsewhere — in the home, with the car and so on.

Reef knot — used for tying sail ties around a furled sail on the boom or tying up a jib. Basically it is just right end over left end and under, then left over right and under. If you get into the habit of doing a reef knot with a tail or loop, it will be easier and quicker to undo. The pressure on the knot will pull the loop in tight. To get the knot undone, all you need do is give the tail a jerk.

Figure-8 knot — more of a twist than a knot, the figure-8 is used in the tails of sheets and halyards to stop them running through a block or fairlead or exitbox. If, for example, you were wanting to get the mainsail down in a hurry in a storm, the main halyard would disappear through the bottom of the mast and out through the top unless you had a figure-8 in the end of it. Similarly, a mainsheet without a figure-8 would disappear through the mainsheet blocks and you'd be without control when suddenly letting go of the main in a big blow. To keep them there permanently — since nobody ever needs to undo them — figure-8s can be sewn in with thread.

1   Holding the short end of the rope towards your body, make a loop in the short end over the top of the long end.

2   Hold the loop firm and then take the short end around the back of the long end.

3   Bring the short end back through the top of the loop. Pull tight.

Figure-8 knot

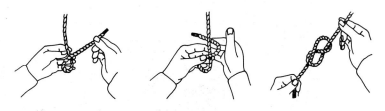

A figure-8 knot is used as a 'stopper' in the end of a sheet or halyard tail.

Clove hitch

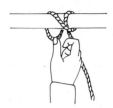

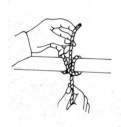

Clove hitch — a quick hitching knot used for tying on flags, sail ties and fenders, for tying up anything temporarily or in a hurry. Not to be used for tying ropes under strain, for example on a dinghy towline: it can become very hard to undo as the strain jams the knot tight. Furled sails can be secured by several long clove hitches.

1   The short end of the rope goes over and around the back of the securing object and crosses over the top of the long end.

2   The short end is taken over and around again with the tail of the short end, then taken under the diagonal crossover.

3   Pull both ends slightly to tighten.

Bowline (pronounced 'bowlin') — the knot yachting revolves around. It is the best multi-purpose knot there is and you can use it to attach jib sheets into the clew of the headsail, to secure a line to a mooring post, to fasten a safety line around someone's chest, or to tie a dinghy painter to an aft cleat. It is easily undone, and of all the knots puts the least strain on the rope. It will not come undone accidentally.

1   Hold the rope over your left hand with the short end towards your body and make a loop over one fingertip (not thumb) with the loop crossing on top . If you're left handed, hold the rope in your right hand.

2   The short end is then passed up through the loop and taken behind the long end. (If you are using the bowline to tie a jib sheet into the clew of the headsail, the short end goes through the clew, then up through the loop.)

3   The short end is then taken back down through the loop. Lock the knot by pulling on the long end.

Bowline

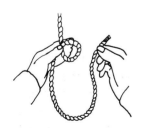 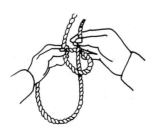 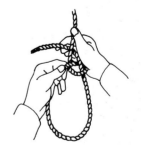 

Tying a bowline into a jib clew: First, a loop is made in the long end of the rope.

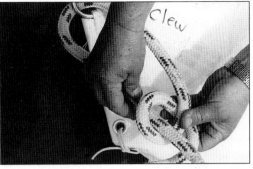

Then the short end is threaded through the clew and up through the loop.

To finish, pass short end around back of loop and then down through it. Short end is pulled to tighten the knot.

cleating ropes

First take the rope around the back of the cleat once, then over it in a figure-8. Finish by taking the rope back behind the cleat twice. Do not use half hitches to tighten it as these are likely to jam on the cleat when the rope is under pressure and you are trying to get it off in a hurry. Half-hitching on a cleat is unnecessary with today's modern ropes.

Photograph shows jib sheet cleated off (when not using a self-tailing winch).

coiling ropes

Loose ropes and halyard tails should always be coiled up out of the way, rather than left lying loose where they can become kinked or knotted, and be a nuisance. Holding one end of the rope in one hand, feed large even loops into that palm with the other hand. Move your hands apart to gather a good length of line then bring them back together to collect the coil, and secure in the gathering hand. Always coil from the secured end.

Never wrap ropes around your elbow because when you come to use them you'll find they have become knotted and twisted and won't pull out cleanly.

Leave a short tail at the end of the coil and take it around the throat of the coil five times then pass the tail through the top of the coil. Give it a bit of a tug to tighten. (Don't take the five turns around the middle of the coil or it goes all floppy.) Now, no matter which end you throw to someone, it will be a simple matter to unwrap the turns and the coil will come out cleanly.

With halyard tails, start from the cleated end, as close to the cleat as possible. When the coils are completed, put your free hand through the front of the coil and take hold of the rope next to the cleat. Pull this back through the coils, and hitch it over the coils and onto the cleat or winch.

Coiling a rope: gather in large, even loops.

Coil the short end around throat of the coil then pass short end through coil throat.

Tug short end to tighten the coil.

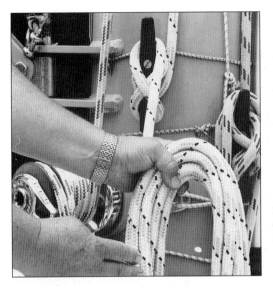

Coiling halyard tail: Coil from cleated end, as close as possible to cleat.

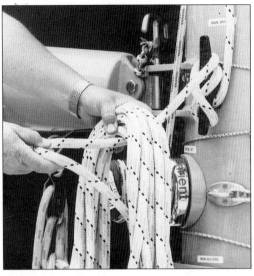

Pass free hand through the coil to grab secured end . . .

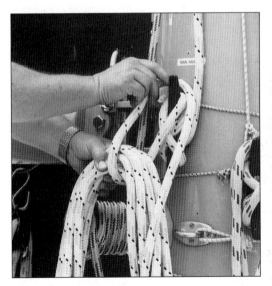

. . . which is pulled through the coil, over the top, and coiled onto cleat.

hurling a line

If you are going to throw a line to someone in trouble, you must take time to check that the coils are evenly laid in your hand and, of course, that the line looks long enough. Then split the coils, keeping the majority in one hand close to the body, and holding the rest in the other throwing hand. Stand side-on to your target, leaning the shoulder opposite to your throwing arm in the direction you're throwing, and brace your legs. Swing your arm back and then swing

Hurling a line: Lay coils evenly in one hand.

Split coils to hold just a few in the throwing hand.

Stand side-on to the direction of the throw and lean shoulder into it.

Swing the whole body into the throw . . .

. . . aiming the rope above your target. Let the balance of the rope go an instant after the throwing coils.

your whole body into the throw. Aim the rope above your goal and let the coils in your non-throwing hand go momentarily after the first coils. It's always a good idea to have your end of the line securely tied to the boat.

splicing

Splicing is a method of making a permanent eye in the end of a rope, or joining two ropes together, by interweaving their strands. It is most often used to make a permanent eye in the end of a rope used as a mooring line, safety harness lanyard, dinghy painter or anchor warp.

To splice an eye, first unstrand the end of a length of 3-ply rope and splay out the strands. These will be woven through the twisted open strands further along the rope. Holding the splayed end away from you, bend the tail under and away from you to form a loop. Twist the rope at that point in the opposite direction to which it is twined — this will open and spread the strands — and push the middle top strand through any of the twisted strands of the twined section. Pull it through tight.

Next, take the rope strand to the left of the one you've just inserted, take it over the strand you pushed the first splayed strand into, and insert it through the next strand. The third remaining strand — on this first round only — is taken back through the eye, over the last twisted-out strand, and through the very next one. This is what makes the eye tight.

Once the strands have all been anchored into the body of the rope in this way you then start with any of the strands and, turning the whole splice towards you, take it over one strand, then under and through the next one. Pull it through tight and proceed with the next strand to left and repeat, turning the splice towards you, over one, under one. Continue until all the strands are woven into the body of the rope. Your spliced eye is complete. Always splice into main core.

Splicing an eye: Middle strand inserted.

Next left strand taken over first strand, then inserted.

Remaining strand taken back through the eye and over.

Completed eye.

sails

parts of the sail

Wools flowing aft indicate correct sheet tension. Halyard tension is insufficient, however, as shown by the scalloping effect on the luff.

In strong winds, mainsail can be flattened by pulling down on block attached to cunningham hole.

A SAIL HAS A head at the top and a foot at the bottom. The edge attached to the mast is the luff and the outside edge with battens, the leach. The tack is the corner of the foot nearest the luff.

Battens are thin, flexible pieces of fibreglass or formica inserted into pockets in the leech of the mainsail to stiffen and support that edge. They are numbered from the head (number 1 at the head) to the foot of the sail and are of varying length.

Wools or tell-tales attached to the luff of the head sail are the cheapest and most effective way to tell if your sails are set correctly when the wind is forward of the beam. Using a needle and 40 to 46 cm of knitting wool, make a hole through the sail about 1.2 metres up the luff and about 46 cm in. Pull the wool through until there's an equal length each side of the sail and tie a knot in each end against the sail. Repeat two or three times more up the luff. Self-adhesive wools can be purchased from a sailmaker.

The cunningham hole is a hole through the sail above the tack and through which a rope tie can be attached and pulled back to the mast in order to gain extra tension on the luff and flatten the sail in strong wind conditions. Always hoist the sail as high as possible first, then pull down on the cunningham hole. It is really a racing control for the sail.

A cringle is an eye in a sail.

Reef points are eyelets, set in the sail for use when reefing down or reducing sail area.

Sails — It is usual for a yacht to carry a wardrobe of sails that includes a mainsail, a selection of headsails for varying wind strengths and a spinnaker for downwind sailing and racing.

There is just the one mainsail, which can be reefed down to reduce sail area in strong winds, but a basic wardrobe of sails will include a number of headsails. While the mainsails of large yachts — with the exception of some three-quarter rigs — are primarily there to provide stability, it is the headsail that provides driving power, and for the yacht to sail efficiently, wind strength must be matched by the appropriate headsail.

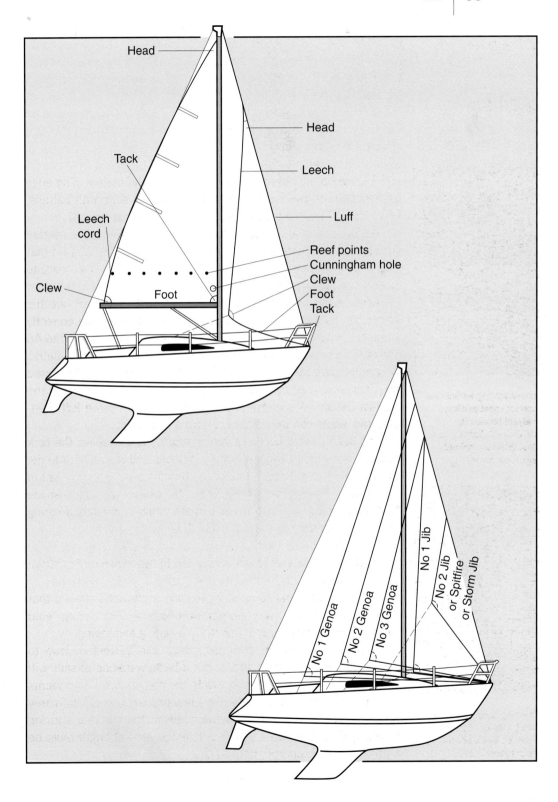

'Mitre' is angle of line from clew to point two-thirds of the way up luff of headsail. Extending line down to deck indicates correct positioning of track slide for that sail.

Where the clew of the headsail overlaps the mainmast, the headsail is called a genoa: if the clew is forward of the mast, the sail is called a jib. The biggest headsail a yacht carries is a No. 1 genoa. Its head is at the top of the sail, the tack is right down near the base of the forestay, and the foot lays along the deck. The No. 1 genoa is used in very light winds, to about 12 knots. In more than 12 knots of wind, it is replaced by a No. 2 genoa, which is shorter on the hoist or luff, and shorter on the foot. This headsail is carried from about 12 to 15 knots of wind when a No. 3 genoa is substituted. This is shorter again on the hoist and foot and is used in up to 15 to 18 knots of wind. A No. 1 jib follows (up to 25 knots of wind), then a No. 2 jib (into 40 knots of wind). As each of the headsails is a different length on the foot, its sheets will be positioned at different places along the headsail track on the sidedecks.

The exact placement of the track slide is determined by the angle of the headsail's mitre. This is the line from about two-thirds of the way up the luff of the sail, through the clew and extending down to the deck. Where the line meets the deck is where the track slide should be. Some headsails are mitre cut and the mitre line is indicated by the mitre seam of the sail. If carrying genoas, the track slide will be well aft; if jibs, the track slides will be well forward.

A spinnaker may be carried any time the wind is aft of the beam to increase boat speed downwind. This sail and its running rigging are set outside any other sails and rigging, and usually used for racing.

sail use

Furling and stowaway sails. In the last few years development in this area has been rapid. It has enabled large keelers to be sailed efficiently with fewer people. Most cruising boats today opt for a furling headsail instead of a wardrobe of genoas and jibs. But roller furling headsails do have limitations. They are hard to pull away in a fresh breeze. When they are reduced, they cannot be flattened like a single hanked-on jib, and the yacht therefore will not point or sail as well. In storm conditions they will need to be rolled completely away, and a small storm jib is needed to be attached to an inner forestay for performance. However, for cruising boats the new generation of furling headsails has given many families who often sail with inexperienced crew aboard greater confidence with their boats in most conditions. I am now demonstrating the uses of a furling headsail in my instruction classes as well as the Hank system.

The stowaway main that rolls away inside the mast or boom is also gaining popularity with boat owners. But for the advantages with this system, you do give away sailing performance. This is quite marked in some conditions. The cost of the stowaway main system is high, as the yacht will need a specially designed and constructed mast, and in smaller keel boats the extra weight and size of the mast will be prohibitive. These mains do not have battens.

The stowaway boom is a further development in this area. Instead of the main rolling away inside the mast, the sail is reduced and stowed by being wound around a special boom. One advantage with this new system is that the main can be fully battened, thus allowing the sail to hold an excellent shape.

You can race with these sails, but for top performance racing the wardrobe of sails is still preferred.

Flaking sails is to fold them up in such a way that they may be stowed compactly and ready for instant rigging with the tack, clew and head easily accessible.

1   Stretch the foot of the sail out tight between the tack and clew.
2   Keeping the tack and clew ends taut, pick up the sail about a metre up the luff and leech, and lay this fold on top of the foot. Repeat this procedure up to the head.
3   Fold the ends of the flaked sail into the middle and roll up tightly from one end. Pack the sail into a sail bag, tie with a sail tie.

Flaking a sail.

Flaking the headsail: Stretch out foot of sail tight between tack and clew. Fold sail, back and forth, concertina-style, over top of foot.

Ends of flaked sail are then folded into middle before rolling up sail, securing with sail tie and packing into sail-bag.

Securing bulk of furled mainsail to the boom with a sail tie.

Like people, sails stretch and sag with age. The sail will still perform adequately but never as efficiently as a new sail. Even lots of outhaul and halyard tensioning won't make a good –looking sail out of an old one.

care of the sail

If you are leaving the boat for a week, wet sails are best left strewn about in the cabin to dry. They may become mouldy if stuffed into bags, or even flaked. Certainly, sails should never be hung out from the mast to dry. The flapping that results will cost you a dollar a flap as stitching is loosened and undone.

Sunlight has a deteriorative effect on sail stitching and if the mainsail is to be left on the boom, use a cover to completely shield the sail, including the clew and head. Acrylic boom covers are best as they allow the air to circulate around the sail. Waterproof covers are not recommended as the sail will sweat under the cover and cause mildew. Ensure the sail is securely tied.

All sails should be regularly inspected for damaged stitching and chafing, especially where they press against fittings or rigging, at seams, reef points, and batten pockets.

If you keep your feet and boat-shoes clean, you'll keep your sails clean and won't ever have to worry about washing off dirty marks — which are mostly caused by dirty shoes. If you have to clean a sail, do it on the boat. Taking the sail home so you can spread it out will only provide more opportunities for dirtying it. You see people on these fools' errands. They bundle up their sails, stuff them in their cars, and then when they've got them home they get grass stains on them and the odd bit of oil from the drive . . . keep your feet clean and you'll never have to worry.

Dirty anchor warps are another cause of grubby sails. Take care when picking up anchors, especially from muddy sea bottoms — get headsails off the deck.

spinnaker

A spinnaker may be carried any time the wind is aft of the beam to increase downwind speed. When cruising, it is usually carried set in light and medium winds. The spinnaker and its running rigging is set outside all other sails and rigging. Today with modern hull and sail shape, yachts go almost as fast with a genoa. A spinnaker is best kept for the racing crew aboard.

Because the spinnaker is flown free with no luff edge that is secured by slides or hanks in position, terminology can be confused. Until it is hoisted, the spinnaker can be described as having a head and two clews, but once set with one end of the foot attached to the spinnaker pole, that corner can then be deemed to be the tack as,

After packing spinnaker, the clew, tack and head can be kept together at top of bag for quick attachment by threading them together on the sail bag tie. Knot with a clove hitch.

like other tacks, it is fixed to something — the pole for example — while the clew corner is free.

A spinnaker pole is used to position the tack of the spinnaker and is itself held in place by a topping lift and downhaul. The windward spinnaker sheet or guy is commonly termed a 'preventer' and is attached to a fitting at the end of the pole and tensioned to prevent the spinnaker pole from hitting the forestay. A pole crashing into the forestay can result in the forestay giving way.

A correct spinnaker set is dependent upon a correctly packed spinnaker. This is done as follows:

1   Gather up the foot of the sail and place this into the sail bag or basket, leaving the tack and clew free. Most spinnakers have a black or white tape edging the foot and coloured tapes on the luffs to be readily identifiable.

2   Gather together each luff from the clew up to the head, and then place the two luffs in the bag, each to its own side of the bag, leaving the head out.

3   Check that the clew, tack and head are still free. Hold them up together, clear of the bag, and stuff the belly of the sail into the bag.

4   Fold the clew and tack over the top of the sail, then head in on top of them.

This packing method eliminates any 'wineglass' twists in the sail when it's hoisted.

multi-purpose sail

These sails are very popular and a very good alternative to a spinnaker. They are easy to rig, set, hoist and take down. They can be carried with the wind forward of the beam, to flat off and running. They are tacked on the bow, usually have only one sheet and are hoisted by the spinnaker halyard inside a tube like a sock, and, in fact, is called a spinnaker sock. Then a light line is pulled and the sock goes to the top of the hoisted sail. This is pulled down before the halyard is lowered. These sails are efficient in up to 15 knots of wind. It is essential to let the sheet go before pulling down the sock.

setting off
— rigging and hoisting

RIG UP AND OTHER preparations for sailing are best done before the boat is moved away from its mooring or, if a trailer sailer, launched from its trailer. It is easier to fit slides to tracks and to do up shackles while the boat is stationary, rather than out at sea with it pitching and rolling. Likewise, it's easier to give a little thought to weather conditions at this stage rather than later when a heavy sea is upon you. Is the headsail you've selected the one best suited to the forecast wind? Is all your gear in good order? Keep in mind that it is a great deal easier to set off under-rigged and then put on bigger sails, than to sail off and have to reduce sail in confined rough waters.

A balanced rig is easy to steer. If this isn't the case, then reef your main or change the headsail as necessary.

rigging the mainsail

1   Unfold the sail and attach the halyard shackle to the head of the sail. (The halyard can be kept handy if attached by a small rope strop to the sidestays, same side as the halyard exit box.)

2   Push the slides on the luff up the mast track.

3   Insert the pin/stop into the bottom of the track to prevent the slides slipping out of the track.

4   Attach the foot of the sail along boom, using slides or ties.

5   Attach the outhaul to the clew of the sail.

6   Attach the gooseneck to the tack with a shackle.

7   Insert battens into the leech of the sail and secure, tying them in with a reef knot.

8   Pull the outhaul tight, and secure the outhaul to the outhaul cleat.

9   To prevent the main halyard twisting and fouling itself around the spreaders while the boat is motoring out of its berth, it is stropped down until you are ready to hoist. Leaving the halyard on the head of the sail, take the wire or rope under

RIGGING THE MAINSAIL

Attach the halyard to head of sail and push slides up mast track.

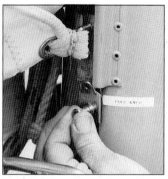

Insert pin-stop into the base of the mast track.

Slide foot of sail along boom track using slides.

Attach outlaul to clew.

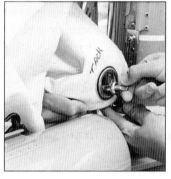

Attach tack of sail to tack shackle on gooseneck. Tighten outhaul.

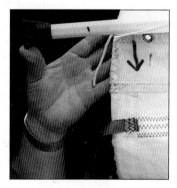

Insert battens into leech.

Furl sail by pulling leech aft and rolling belly of sail into itself.

the top cleat or winch on the boom, then pull your rope halyard tight so the halyard is stropped and not loosely flying about.

10   To keep the sail from flopping about while motoring away from your mooring, it is furled and tied to the boom. Working from the side of the boom that the sail is gathered, furl the sail, by pulling the leech aft and rolling the sail into itself. Ensure it is tight and neat.

11   Using sail ties, tie the sail to the boom with reef knots.

rigging the headsail

1. Unfold the sail and attach the tack to the tack shackle or snap clip at the bottom of the forestay. Preferably attach the tack to a strop 200 mm long or so if using a small headsail. (Only the No. 1 genoa is attached directly to the stem, all other headsails should be on a strop.)

2. Clip the luff of the headsail onto the forestay with the hanks. Always work from the tack to the head and take care not to twist the hanks around or you won't be able to pull the headsail up.

3. Furl the sail and secure with a reef-knotted sail tie to the lifelines. This prevents it flying around and obscuring your vision while you are motoring out.

4. The jib halyard is not attached to the head until you are ready to hoist the sail. This prevents the halyard twisting and fouling. (To prevent mooring lines and/or anchor warps from dirtying furled headsails, tie the sail to the top of the lifelines.)

5. To attach the jib sheets to the clew of the headsail, work from the cockpit, first taking the ends of the sheets through the block by the winches (or if you have fairleads, otherwise simply round the winch), then through the blocks on the jib sheet track slides. Take the sheets outside the sidestays to the headsail. Attach the sheets to the clew with bowlines. Modern beamy yachts sheet jib sheets inside the stays; genoa sheets are run outside.

6. Tie figure-8 knots into the other ends of the jib sheets. From the secured ends of the sheets, coil the tails of the sheets in big even loops and place in the cockpit. Do not cleat them.

Make sure the sheets are not chafing on any hard corners and check the track slide position for the size of headsail you are carrying.

Roller-furling headsails are increasingly popular on all sizes of yachts. Not only does such a sail make for easier sailing but also means you don't need to carry so many separate sails.

RIGGING THE HEADSAIL

Attach tack to shackle at stemhead.

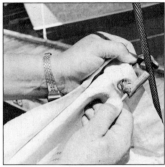

Hank luff to forestay, ensuring hanks are all the right way around.

Secure furled headsail with sail ties.

Jib sheet is reeved through block on jib sheet track.

Take jib sheet outside sidestays.

Use bowlines to tie jib sheets into clew of headsail. And tie figure-8 knots in the ends of jib sheets.

hoisting the mainsail

1   With the engine in neutral, head directly into the wind before hoisting.
2   Remove sail ties.
3   Uncleat and really free the mainsheet in the cockpit.
4   Let the boom vang go. Unstrop the main halyard from its boom cleat. Check it is running free.
5   Hoist the sail by pulling it up hand-over-hand before putting it on the winch. When the sail is almost at the top, put the halyard onto the main halyard winch drum, putting on plenty of turns so you can get lots of halyard tension. Winch for full tension then cleat the halyard. Most boats will have the exit box for the main halyard at about head height or higher. This allows you to pull down on it hand-over-hand, which is a lot more natural and effective than pulling up on a rope. The odd boat has the exit box at the bottom of the mast, and this makes the job difficult. The more wind there is, the more tension should be applied to the halyard.

HOISTING THE MAINSAIL

Main halyard is pulled down hand over hand, using power of shoulders and back.

Halyard is wound onto drum of winch, then . . .

. . . one crew keeps tension on halyard tail — called tailing — while another winches.

With the mainsail hoisted, uncleat and lower main topping lift to take tension off the boom.

hoisting the headsail

1   The headsail is hoisted once you are on your course. Otherwise, if you tried hoisting the headsail while heading into the wind, the sail and jib sheets would fly around and make things both difficult and potentially harmful. This is another reason I prefer knots in the ends of jib sheets rather than clips into the headsail clew.
2   Remove sail ties.
3   Ease the jib halyard at the mast.
4   Attach the jib halyard to head of sail with a snap clip.
5   Ensure the jib sheets are free then hoist, using the winch for tensioning.
6   Cleat the jib halyard.
7   Only sheet in when halyard tension is gained.

Once the sails are hoisted, check their tension. To be most effective, the tension on the outhaul and on the halyards of both sails must be enough to allow the sails to set smooth and tight, like aeroplane wings. Horizontal creases in the luffs of the sails indicate insufficient halyard tension; if the foot of the main is scallopy and loose, the outhaul has not been pulled tight enough. It is always easier to ease an over-tensioned halyard than to tighten a loose one. The majority of people underhoist their boats' sails, and accordingly, don't sail as effectively as they could.

Remember: Light wind — light tension, medium wind — medium tension, hard strong wind — hard tension.

You generally find that if rigging is hard work, then you're doing something wrong. Strength is rarely needed on a boat, but you must know how to use your weight. When hoisting, for example, don't try and do it all in your forearms, but swing down with full armlengths, using your shoulders and back. If for some reason it is hard, or you can't work something out, stop and have a look and a think — chances are it will all become clear, or you'll see what has become caught up.

HOISTING THE HEADSAIL

Remove sail ties.

Attach jib halyard to head with snap-clip and hoist the sail.

Take halyard onto winch once headsail is raised, using the self-tailer.

Winching.

Cleat halyard after headsail is correctly tensioned on winch (if you don't have a self-tailer).

hoisting the spinnaker

At the bow:

1   Take the bag or basket to the bow and tie it on the forestay, preferably in front of the forestay or otherwise just behind it to leeward.
2   Clip the windward sheet/preventer into the tack and then put it through the end of the pole. The preventer is always to windward to hold the pole from hitting the forestay.
3   Clip the leeward sheet into the clew.
4   Just before you are ready to hoist, attach the spinnaker halyard. Ensure that everything is set outside the forestay, headsail, pulpit.

At the mast:

1   Slacken the spinnaker halyard.
2   Undo the spinnaker topping lift and attach it to the pole, preferably with the jib sheet over the pole.
3   Take up the topper (topping lift) so the pole is just above the pulpit.
4   When ready on the bow (the preventer has been attached) take up the topper until the pole is level with the horizon or the main boom.
5   When all is ready aft, hoist the sail as fast as possible, and get it onto the winch quickly and cleated before the spinnaker sheet is pulled in. This is a huge sail and once it fills with wind the pressure on sheet and halyard is enormous; if the sheet is pulled in before the halyard is cleated, the person at the mast will be pulled up into the air, hanging onto the end of the halyard.

With the spinnaker hoisted, drop the headsail as soon as possible. The headsail should always be up before you hoist a spinnaker as it will help prevent the spinnaker twisting or wrapping itself around the forestay. Before you take the spinnaker down, rehoist the headsail.

The spinnaker pole always goes to the windward side of the boat, usually as a continuation of the main boom, and is carried square to the wind. If the wind is dead aft, the pole will be all the way aft nearly at right-angles to the beam. If the wind is coming halfway between the beam and stern, the pole will be out halfway between beam and bow. When the wind is on the beam, the pole will be

In this view, braided ropes clipped horizontally are spinnaker sheets, single different patterned rope is spinnaker downhaul.

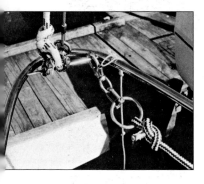

Detail photograph shows rope spinnaker halyard attached vertically to pulpit (to left of wire jib halyard). Snap-clipped horizontally to pulpit is one of the spinnaker sheets. White knotted line looped to release pin of snap shackle is trip line (knots provide operator with grip).

HOISTING THE SPINNAKER

Topping lift clipped to spinnaker pole. Leeward jib sheet is laid over top of pole.

Parrot beak at inboard end of pole attaches to fitting on mast.

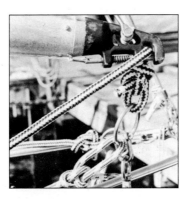

Connecting outboard parrot beak to windward jib sheet. The pole is butted up against the knot.

Attaching halyard to head of spinnaker.

After raising the pole, the spinnaker topping lift is tensioned and cleated.

Spinnaker set: note parrot beak butted up to windward side of windward sheet knot.

Hoisting the spinnaker: spinnaker bag tied on at bow.

The spinnaker is clipped on, and the pole topped up and brought aft with the preventer.

Spinnaker hoisted.

Rubber-bands (see p.51) hold spinnaker from blowing out immediately.

almost touching the forestay. Never allow the pole to touch the forestay.

If on occasion the crew have a hard time hoisting the spinnaker, you should bear off until downwind so that the mainsail will blanket the spinnaker. Continue downwind until the spinnaker is hoisted, then attempt to go back onto course.

Working the downhaul — while the topping lift holds the spinnaker pole up, the downhaul or foreguy holds the pole down or level. It is used with the preventer to keep the pole properly positioned. The person on the downhaul works in conjunction with the crew on the preventer: if the downhaul is being eased, the preventer must be pulled in, and vice versa. Downhaul out, preventer in; preventer in, downhaul out — all the time making sure that the pole is kept level and not waving about with slack on the downhaul.

Working the preventer — the preventer, or preventer brace or afterguy, stops the spinnaker pole hitting the forestay. The ideal is to keep the pole always square to the wind. This means its position will range from being near the forestay when the wind is abeam to being pulled all the way back when the wind is aft.

Working the sheet — the sheet controls the spinnaker as it pulls in and eases the spinnaker clew, to catch the wind and so drive the yacht. Keep plenty of flow on the sheet, winding it in and easing it out as necessary to play the wind. To trim your sheet, watch the luff edge between pole and head: this edge should be kept just at the point of collapse.

The jib halyard has been released and the headsail is starting to come down.

Spinnaker starts to set as rubber-bands are torn away by the filling sail.

Headsail now all the way down . . . and spinnaker full.

Running downwind.

When the spinnaker comes down, the sheet is cleated and the sail is pulled aboard under the mainsail and into the cockpit.

Photograph shows spinnaker sheet passing through tweaker. Tweaker is used to pull down leech of spinnaker and so flatten the sail. This prevents the sail filling totally in the leech and stops the boat rolling.

lowering the spinnaker

1   Hoist the headsail.
2   Ease the preventer to allow the pole to go forward to trip the sail from the preventer (not the preventer from the pole). As the preventer is eased, the downhaul will be pulled in as the pole goes forward.
3   Cleat leeward sheet.
4   Keeping the pole from hitting the forestay, trip the spinnaker from the leeward side of the bow, then uncleat and lower the halyard.
5   Pull the spinnaker aboard from under the mainsail.
6   Attach the halyard and sheet together and pull forward with the downhaul. Uncleat the sheets, preventer and downhaul.
7   Attach gear back onto pulpit.
8   Lower topping lift and detach topper and pole.
9   Recleat halyard and topper at mast.

Tripping the spinnaker can be dangerous if your head is to either side of the pole. A safe procedure is to place yourself on the leeward side of the headsail and forestay and reach around the forestay to trip the sail from the clip (not the pole), leaving the sheet in the pole. If you have to be on the windward side, keep yourself well clear of the pole as you trip it: the pole will fly aft if there is too much weight on the preventer and not enough weight on the downhaul, or it will fly forward if the preventer is too loose. Any time you trip the pole, make sure your course is well downwind as the further forward the wind is, the more weight there is on the pole. If wanting to trip the spinnaker because of an approaching heavy squall or during strong winds that threaten to rip the sail, undo the figure-8 knot in the preventer and let it go. The sheet will run out through the parrot beak and the spinnaker can be pulled in under the mainsail.

Most of the time, in light to moderate winds, you will be able to free-fly the spinnaker out of the sail bag or basket as outlined above. But when it is blowing hard or gusting — or you are sailing shorthanded — it is preferable to have some kind of control on the spinnaker as it's hoisted, so it doesn't twist or wrap itself around the forestay. One method is to loop rubber-bands over the spinnaker, or tie lengths of knitting wool around it (do not use acrylic wool), so it is banded together like a string of sausages. The sail is hoisted like this and once it is cleated the two sheets are pulled in, the rubber-

In strong wind conditions the spinnaker can be rubber-banded before it is hoisted, to prevent it being tangled in the standing rigging. Rubber-bands are slid onto the sail every metre or so as it is pulled out of the bag. If the rubber-bands won't break as the spinnaker is hoisted, a pull on the leeward sheet will help them on their way.

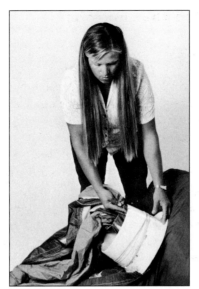 

bands fly off, and the spinnaker is left sitting pretty.

You will need a large plastic bucket from which the bottom has been cut out. Turn the bucket upside down so the hole is now at the top and stretch over it a number of rubber-bands. Now place the inverted bucket over the top of the sail bag or basket and pull the head of the spinnaker through it while holding together the two luffs further down. Pull out about a metre of sail — the two luff edges held together — and slide on a rubber-band from the bucket. Pull out another metre of sail and slide on another rubber band. Continue for the length of the sail.

chapter 6

sailing theory and techniques

A YACHT SAILS in much the same way that an aeroplane flies. Air passing over a curved surface has the effect of creating a low pressure area above it and in a practical application this results in the aeroplane lifting up into the relative vacuum created by the low pressure area. Similarly, a yacht is pulled forward ahead of the sail.

The best guide to wind angle is an arrow or flag attached to the top of the mast. Pieces of wool tied to the sidestays are also helpful. Your wind indicator is the most important piece of equipment on the whole boat. Using it, you will be able to work out where the wind is coming from, what tack you are on, and at what angle the sails should be.

The wind is one force being exerted on a yacht, the weight of the keel is another. Wind pushing against a boat's sails is counteracted by the resistance of the keel through the water, so that instead of the boat being pushed over, the keel keeps it upright or at an angle reducing sideways movement and helping to convert the energy into forward movement.

When pulled in, the mainsail applies the greatest leverage on the keel and the boat heels over. When the mainsail is eased the boat sails at a flatter angle. (In a strong gust of wind, letting the mainsheet go will result in the boat sitting up flat in an instant. This can be practised a couple of times to encourage the confidence of family or friends aboard.)

The headsail, on the other hand, is the keeler's driving force, its aeroplane wing-like shape pulling the boat forward.

When we are talking about wind direction, it is more practical to think of it in terms of the boat than as points of the compass. The wind is onto the boat from one of three places: forward of the beam, on the beam, or aft of the beam. In determining the optimum angle your sails should be set at, given the angle of the wind on the boat, try to imagine the face of a clock superimposed over the boat. At the bow is 12; 1, 2 and 3 from the bow back to the beam on the starboard; 4 and 5 aft of the beam; 6 on the stern. Now imagine dividing the two sides of the boat into two 30-minute sections. Use the arrow at the top of the mast as a minute hand and treat the wind over the starboard side ('past the hour'), the same as wind over the

Swedish Windex 15 wind-direction indicator not only shows direction of wind, but its display is so constructed that a helmsman can readily note even a small change in the apparent wind angle. Indicator has reflective underside for night reading and the tails are set at 5-to and 5-past for on the wind.

Trimming sails by the clock method. The boom when all the way out cannot sit at right angles because of the sidestays. <u>Your arrow points into the wind.</u>

'Aim for sailing that is efficient and effective.'

'The sails are in when you can't pull them in any more.'

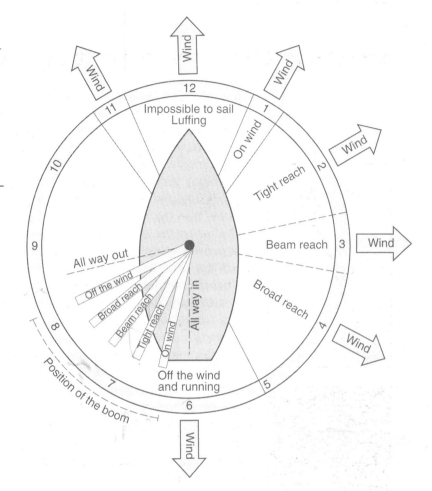

port side ('before the hour'). Relate the position of the arrow to fractions of the half hour and set your sails accordingly, keeping in mind that the sails work through a 15-minute arc. If the wind is coming over the boat at '5 minutes to the hour' (that is, on the port side), both the mainsail and headsail should be 5/30 of the way out (on the starboard side: the boat is on the wind). If the wind is 15 minutes to the hour, both sails should be 15/30 of the way out (that is, halfway out: beam reach). If the arrow indicates the wind at about 25 past, then both sails need to be out 25/30, which, because of the boom hitting the sidestays, means the boom would, in fact, be almost all the way out. As the wind comes aft the sails go out.

Fluttering, dancing wools on windward side of the headsail indicate that the sail is too slack. Pull in the jib sheet until . . .

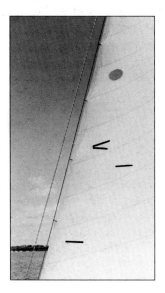

. . . sail is correctly adjusted and wools flow aft.

trimming the sails

In addition to the general setting of the sails, of course, you are always trying to trim them to maximum efficiency — to have them, as mentioned above, with even curves just like aeroplane wings. If they have humps, bumps, crinkles or pleats in them, they are just plain wrong. Nor should they flap and twitter.

Vertical creases in the luffs of the sails indicate too much halyard tension. If the foot of the main is scallopy and loose, the outhaul has not been pulled tight enough.

The wools will only give an indication when the wind is forward of the beam. If the wools on both sides are streaming aft, the sail is correctly adjusted. If one or the other side's wools are 'dancing', however, then the sail, to be correctly trimmed, needs adjustment.

Sailing on the wind — if the windward wools are fluttering, the boat is pointing too high. If the leeward ones, then the boat is too far off the wind. Reaching — if the windward wools are 'dancing', the headsail should be pulled in a little. If the leeward wools, the sail is too taut (you can remember this by remembering: 'inside wools, sail in; outside wools, sail out'.).

Luffing is perhaps the most obvious indication that your sails are incorrectly trimmed, the luff edges of the sails collapsing because wind is getting behind them. This is easily corrected by pulling in the sheets or changing course. If the leech is flapping, it means either the sail is old or the leech cord needs tightening.

steering

When sailing, a yacht's course is relative 'up' or 'down' to the wind. 'Up' means towards the wind, 'down' means away from the wind.

The commands 'Bring her up', 'Up a bit', and 'Higher' all mean to steer the boat up towards the wind. 'Bear away' and 'You're too high' both mean to steer away from the wind.

It's possible, along certain shores, to get lifts or breaks in the direction of the wind. A lift will allow you to point a higher course, and you should take advantage of it because there is bound to be a break-off at some stage before the destination is reached, which will require you to fall off your planned course. Every little puff of wind is coming from a slightly different direction and the clever helmsman will take every opportunity to make ground where he or she can.

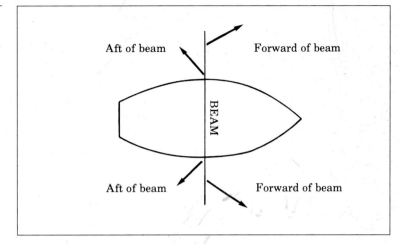

Aft of beam   Forward of beam

BEAM

Aft of beam   Forward of beam

In a keeler, which is steered by a wheel, it is just like driving a car — you simply turn the wheel the way you want to go. Using a tiller is the opposite; from the windward side of the tiller, you push it away from the direction you are wanting to take.

The windward side of the boat is the side nearest where the wind is coming from. The leeward (pronounced 'lewid') side is where the wind is going. Always walk along the decks on the windward side, as this is the high side and you will be on a more comfortable angle. Movement is easier and you can lean down to work, rather than reaching up.

The beam is the middle of a boat and the widest part. All terms relating to the yacht are referred to as forward of beam, aft of beam, and on the beam.

With the wind forward of the beam, the boat is on a port tack when the wind is coming over its port side, and a starboard tack when it is coming over its starboard side (and the boom is out to port). This means the wind is on the opposite side to the main boom.

When the wind is aft, and the mainsail is not necessarily on a different side to the wind, we use the same definition to work out our tack. For example, if the wind is right aft starboard and the sail is starboard, the boat is said to be on a port tack (the tack being opposite to the side the main boom is out).

Winch handle should be kept in pocket whenever it's not in use. A handle knocked overboard is not only inconvenient but also expensive.

winches

Winches are a most necessary aid in gaining sheet or halyard tension. When you are pulling in a sail, the sheet is on the winch

Spinning off leeward sheet: Uncleat sheet and maintain tension on it as the boat is turned into its new tack. Lean back into it.

When headsail starts to luff — when the bow is head to wind — quickly spin off sheet, keeping spinning hand above the drum. Lean in.

The sheet is off the drum and thrown away.

drum all the time; but when you are hoisting a sail, the halyard is pulled down hand-over-hand until it is up, and then it goes onto the winch.

In using a sheet winch, the sheet is first wound three times around the winch, this lead-on being important to prevent the sheet riding or jamming. Never try pulling in a sail without first putting three turns of the sheet on the winch — you need the advantage the winch gives. The fourth turn stops it slipping.

Pull in the sheet hand-over-hand until it becomes too heavy, then put another turn on the winch and have someone else wind it in using the winch handle until the sail is correctly trimmed. Then cleat the sheet.

Make a habit of spinning the drum so you know which way it turns and which way the sheet or halyard should be wound. (Arrows on top of the winch indicate which way it turns.) Always pull a sheet or halyard from behind the winch, never in front as this will cause over-riding.

To ease a sheet or halyard you must retain tension on the sheet after it is uncleated, and then guide it carefully off the winch drum using your fingers and pulling the rope slightly outwards and up to prevent jamming or twists. Don't take turns off.

Never leave the handle unattended in the winch; always keep your hand on it or put it in its pocket. These handles are not only necessary but expensive items, and it is amazing how easily they can go over the side. Taking the handle out and putting it away is a good

Heading into the wind before hoisting the mainsail.

Main halyard is pulled hand over hand, using the power of shoulders and back.

Halyard goes on to the drum and the luff is winched tight. The yacht is still held head to wind.

When the main halyard has been winched tight, the main topping lift is eased to lower the boom.

When the sheet is being winched, the sheet is first wound three times around the winch drum. Once the sheet has been pulled in hand-over-hand as much as possible, a further turn should be added around the winch before using the winch handle.

Headsail here is set correctly, as shown by the wools on the outside of the sail *flowing* aft. In this picture the jib is in use: the roller-furler headsail is rolled up in front of the stay.

After any manoeuvre the jib sheet should be coiled neatly and placed off the cockpit floor.

Spinnaker clews are ready to be attached to the sheets and preventer. Downhaul is visible on the underside of the spinnaker pole.

When spinnaker is held in a sock, the spinnaker is hoisted completely and the halyard cleated before the sock is pulled up the spinnaker.

Here the sock is being raised to allow the spinnaker to fly free.

Spinnaker is set and the spinnaker pole is being pulled aft.

GYBING

Mainsheet has been pulled in, in readiness for a controlled gybe.

Now the boat has changed course and the main has been quickly eased out.

Boom preventer has been pulled in on the port spinnaker winch to hold the boom out and to prevent the boat from rolling.

GOING ABOUT

From a starboard tack: All of the turns of the sheet are left on the winch until the bow of the boat is into the wind . . .

. . . at which time all of the turns are quickly spun off.

Going about is now complete and the crew is doing the final trimming of the headsail. During the going about manouvre the main sheet has been pulled in to bring the boat higher up into the wind.

Sailing is easy if you first get the basics right. And the basics are easily learnt.

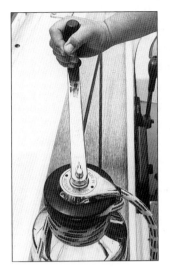

Winching: Sheet is first wound three times around winch drum. When sheet has been pulled in hand-over-hand as much as possible. One more turn will stop the sheet slipping on the drum. Tension is maintained on sheet while another crew cranks the winch with winch handle.

habit to get into, even with the 'lock-in' types.

The tail of a jib sheet is the excess sheet you pull in. To tail a sheet is to take the weight of the sheet while someone else winches. Freeing the tail means getting rid of the jib sheet so that it cannot get caught on blocks, fairleads or shrouds.

Apparent wind is the combined effect of the true wind and the wind made by the movement of the boat. You can see the difference in the two wind directions by comparing the direction of the waves (blown by the true wind) and the direction the mast arrow points to.

The apparent wind seems strongest when the boat is on the wind (as the two winds combine in more or less the same direction), and lightest when sailing away aft of beam or downwind, when the speed of the true wind is partly countered by the boat wind. The apparent wind is felt a few degrees forward of true.

If sailing downwind, the true wind is always stronger than it feels, and in turning back into the wind you should be aware that in heavy weather it may be best to reduce sail.

So, going upwind you deduct boat speed to get true wind speed, and going downwind you add it on. While the boat is moving the wind can often be referred to by its apparent strength as that is what the wind speed indicator is reading. If the reading was say, 40 knots apparent on a broad reach or running, then by adding on boat speed you would know the true wind to be very strong; but if 40 knots apparent on the wind, then the true wind speed is probably about 34 knots.

Apparent wind is the deflected wind resulting from your boat moving across or against the true wind. Sails must be set in relation to the apparent wind and not the true wind, and the direction of apparent wind is found out by looking at the masthead arrow. A yacht only sails in apparent wind. Wools attached to the shrouds can also be used to tell the direction of apparent wind, but are only useful when steering to windward: off the wind, the masthead arrow must be consulted.

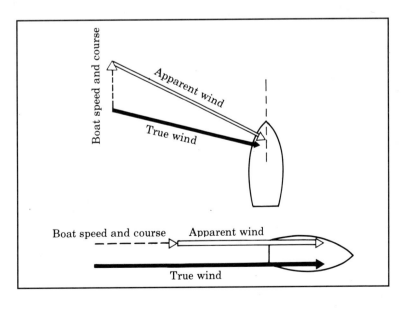

points of sailing

The use of a clockface is helpful in understanding points of sailing. So that with the wind on the beam the sails must be 15/30 (15 minutes of 30 minutes) of the way out — halfway out.

Page 58

All the way in

1/3 of the way out

1/2 way out

2/3 way out

All the way out

On the wind — the closest angle it is possible to sail to the wind is about 30° from the wind (by the clock method, '5 past' or '5 to'). This is the most difficult and challenging point of sailing: the boat is heeling and you are 'beating', 'bashing', 'slogging', 'tacking' or 'on the wind'. Both sails are pulled in tight and while there is a sense of speed, you are travelling more slowly than if on a tight or broad reach.

Tight reach — from between 6 to 13 minutes past (35° to 77° from the wind). The sheets have been eased slightly giving the sails more shape and more drive; the fastest and easiest point of sailing.

Beam reach — 13 to 16 minutes past (77° to 96°). Here you are sailing across the wind with the sails halfway out. If the sails luff, they're out too far: let the sheet out until the sails are on the point of luffing and then pull them in just a little.

Broad reach — 16 to 25 minutes past (96° to 150°). Sailing with the wind with the sails well eased almost all of the way out. The mainsail tends to blanket the headsail, but you can't do anything about this. Tighten the boom vang so that the boom will be held down.

Off the wind, or running — 25 to 30 minutes past (150° to 180°). The wind is directly aft and the sails are eased as far out as possible. The boom will be at right-angles to the yacht, and you are liable to jibe if a good course is not steered.

On the wind.

Beam reach.

Broad reach.

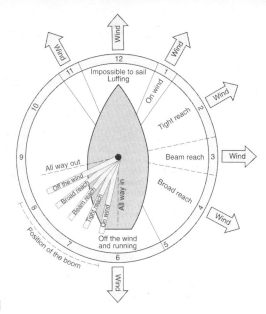

sailing to windward

No boat in the world can sail directly into the wind. In the early days of sailing craft, square-riggers sailed at 90 degrees to the wind because of the shape of the sails but today's cruising yachts can sail between 35 to 40 degrees off the wind.

At this point of sailing, the boat is beating towards the wind, sailing a zig-zag course on alternate tacks. It is the hardest and least comfortable point: the boat is heeled over, the sails are hard aboard and the helmsman has to have a sensitive touch in order to sail course most efficiently.

The aim is to point as high as possible while keeping the fastest possible speed through the water. While pointing the boat higher than this might be more direct, your speed will be slower. A faster speed will be obtained by bearing away, but the boat will have to cover more ground to reach the same destination. However, this is often preferable for reasons of comfort. Remember that the most important thing is to go where you want to go, and to set the sails to suit.

Tacking the boat, sailing it to windward by a series of alternate tacks, enables you to make for a windward destination.

There are two ways of turning a boat: by going about and by gybing. In going about the bow is turned through the eye of the wind. In gybing, the stern is passed through the wind. Depending on wind strength and the direction you want to take, you can either go about or gybe to change tack. However, it is advisable to go about when the wind is forward of the beam and gybe when it is aft of the beam. Gybing is much faster than going about, but because it is faster it can also be more dangerous if you are not prepared for it.

going about

As a reminder of the difference between going about and gybing, you could try:

'About . . . about, about, about, a bow into the wind'.

When the helmsman is ready to change tack he or she will advise the crew of this intention by the call 'Ready about!'

At the point of swinging the helm over to change tack, the helmsman will then call either 'Lee O!', 'About ship!', or 'Helms-a-lee!'

After the helmsman has called 'Ready about!' and is preparing to change tack, the crew see to the following:

1   Uncleat the leeward jib sheet and hold firmly with all of the turns still on the winch.

2   Ready the windward jib sheet by putting three turns on the winch and then pull it taught. One of the crew holds the sheet tail taut and another stands ready with the winch handle.

3   The mainsheet stays cleated. The mainsheet would be adjusted only if you were changing course considerably. If it is necessary to change setting, it is easiest to do this at the point that the sail collapses and there is no pressure on the mainsheet.

4   As the boat is turned into the wind the headsail will luff and that is the cue for the person on the leeward jib sheet to spin all the turns off and let it go. Only when the sail has luffed and the pressure is off the leeward sheet should the crew throw the turns off the winch. If the sheet is hard to spin off and there's pressure on it, then it's being done at the wrong time, either too early or too late.

5   Once the leeward sheet is free and the wheel has been turned or the tiller put hard over, pull in the windward sheet quickly. When all the slack has been taken up by pulling the sheet over the winch by hand put an extra turn on the winch, keep the tension on the sheet and winch in until the headsail is trimmed. Cleat off the sheet. (In strong wind it may be necessary to add one more turn around the winch just before the handle goes on.)

The helmsman firms up on the new course. If on a trailer sailer, the crew will move across to the windward side of the boat again to help balance the boat. This is not necessary on a keel yacht.

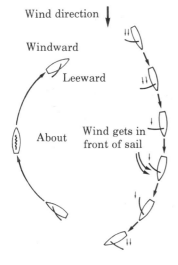

Wind direction

Windward

Leeward

About   Wind gets in
front of sail

Going about and gybing.

GOING ABOUT

From a starboard tack, beam reach. Three turns of the sheet were put on the winch as the helmsman turned bow of the boat into the wind. Now the bow is headed into wind, the leeward sheet has been spun off and the windward sheet is being pulled in on the winch.

On a port tack, tight reach, three turns on the windward winch. Now the helmsman has turned bow into the wind and the crew spins off leeward sheet as the headsail luffs.

Bow continues to move through the wind. One crew attends to the new leeward sheet while the other pulls in mainsheet to position the mainsail for boat's new course.

As boom crosses athwartships the windward sheet is pulled in hand-over-hand on the winch.

Going about completed, the boat now on a port tack. The helmsman is firming up the new course and crew are ready for another tack.

Manoeuvre complete. Crew on leeward sheet eases sheet for correct adjustment of headsail.

gybing

This method of changing direction is faster than going about but it can be more difficult. In a gybe the helmsman turns the bow towards the main boom (instead of towards the wind) and the stern (not the bow) passes through the wind.

The same steps are followed as for going about except that the helmsman's calls will include the word gybe (for example 'Ready to gybe!', 'Gybe-o!'). Also, the cue for letting the leeward jib sheet go will be when the stern crosses the wind and the headsail collapses (same as going about).

Although an uncontrolled gybe — one in which the boom swings across unhindered from one side of the boat to the other — can be accomplished safely in light winds, it is perhaps prudent to get into good habits early and make every gybe a controlled gybe. In this case the mainsheet is pulled in to the centre on the command 'Ready to gybe!' and held, and then as the stern passes through the eye of the wind, the mainsheet is eased out again, quickly but firmly, hand over hand. Never gybe until the mainsail is aboard. As soon as the boat starts turning it will be easier.

In an uncontrolled or flying gybe, mainsheet tension is not applied and the boom swings wildly from one side to the other. Gear failure is possible. A controlled gybe should be done whenever the wind is greater than about 10 knots.

The faster the mainsheet is eased, the easier it will be for the helmsman, because the mainsail is steering the boat.

In tacking, the aim is to keep the highest possible speed throughout the manoeuvre . . . which means tacking fast. A rapid tack can stall a boat, but only if the sails are poorly set. The ideal speed is one that allows the boat to maintain speed as she turns and awaits the filling of her sails on the other side. Practise tacking speeds to gauge which is best for your boat and crew.

A boat that stalls head-to-wind, while tacking, is said to be 'in irons'. To make way again, all sails should be sheeted hard aboard and the helm held hard over to one side. To avoid getting into irons, put the boat about faster, or if a multihull, hold the jib sheet until almost back-winding.

sailing downwind

The further aft the wind comes, the further out the sails will be. However, with the wind directly aft (off the wind, or running) there

GYBING

From a port tack, tight reach. Helmsman turning away from the wind towards boom, crew at the ready.

From a port tack, beam reach. Sheet is being spun off while the other crew pulls in mainsheet to control the gybe.

Stern passes through the wind, boom moves across. Crew on leeward sheet keeps it tensioned.

Boom now passing over the cockpit. Last turn of the jib sheet is spun off the leeward winch.

Gybed. Leeward sheet and mainsheet being eased to adjust headsail and mainsail. Horizon in this sequence shows how the bow has moved away from the wind (left of bridge) to downwind.

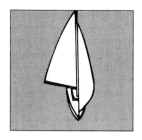

Sailing goose-winged.

is the danger of accidental gybing. In fluky conditions especially, an inexperienced helmsman may inadvertently allow the wind to cross from one side of the stern to the other and force the mainsail to crash across, possibly damaging gear and injuring crew.

Involuntary gybes can be guarded against by steering a few degrees off dead aft so the wind comes across on the quarter opposite the mainsail. It may be necessary in this case to tack downwind on long broad reaches to keep on course, but the extra boat speed achieved will make up for the slightly longer distance that has to be covered.

As well, because the boat is more likely to roll with the wind aft, and because it is possible for it to roll itself into a gybe, the boom vang should be tightened. This will hold the boom down, which in turn will keep the leech straight and flat. It is when the leech of the sail is floppy that the boat will roll. Also, a boom preventer prevents the boom from flying about in a gybe and stops a boat rolling. As well, it should be attached to a strong point at the outboard end on the boom vang, taken through any block on the leeward rail and then cleated off in the cockpit, so that if the boat accidentally gybes, the boom will be restrained and the helmsman has time to adjust course.

The yacht can also be steadied by poleing the headsail out to the side opposite the mainsail, so it is 'goose-winged'. This requires a competent helmsman to prevent an uncontrolled gybe. If the wind increases, this setting can be maintained by reducing sail area as before — through changing the headsail and reefing the main.

In strong downwind sailing, the crew should move aft — and distribute themselves evenly on each side of the boat — to balance the effect of the wind pushing on the sails and forcing the bow down.

When sailing downwind in light conditions, never be tempted to tie the main boom to the sidestays. Use a preventer. If land distorts your wind or the wind suddenly changes, you may gybe, and if the boom is tied out to the then wrong side, the boat is unmanageable.

Again, with the wind aft in light conditions, you could pole out the genoa. You need a topping lift on the pole and you run one sheet through the end of the pole and sheet it aft. The other jib sheet is used for a downhaul to keep the pole level at all times.

sail trim and adjustment

On all points of sailing the ideal is for the boat to be sailed as

Unless you are in top-level racing, the mainsheet traveller should always be positioned amidships and not allowed to fly across from side to side of the cockpit or cabin top. If the wind is strong and the boat or mainsail is hard to handle, then the traveller can be set to leeward to spill more wind from the main.

Poled-out genoa has topping lift attached to its centre. Jib sheet acting as downhaul runs from outboard end of pole forward to bow. Windward jib sheet runs aft to cockpit. When carrying a spinnaker in strong wind, the bow is pulled down and the stern lifts. In certain conditions the stern will lift and the boat will heel to such a degree that rudder control is lost and the boat broaches. To avoid a broach, sail a lower course and let the mainsheet go. Someone should be on the mainsheet at all times when flying a spinnaker in such conditions.

effectively as possible. This involves helmsman and crew in a continual appraisal of wind and sea conditions, and set of the sails. Once on course, both the main and jib sheets can be eased out until the sails just begin to flutter. They are then pulled in just beyond the point where they stop fluttering, that is, luffing. Now they should be operating (like aeroplane wings) at their most efficient.

If the wind moves forward or aft, tighten or ease the sheets accordingly, so the angle of the wind on the boat is reflected in the setting of the sails.

If the wind increases, you will have to consider changing the headsail to one of smaller size and/or reefing the main. You will also probably need to tighten the halyards.

Sailing downwind with a poled-out genoa.

changing sails

the mainsail

THE HARDER THE WIND blows, the less sail you require to maintain the boat's maximum controlled speed. In order to maintain control and reduce the heel and power of the boat in heavy weather, the mainsail will also have to be reduced in area. Instead of changing it for a smaller sail, as with the headsail, the main is reefed down to one of its three sets of reef points. It is lowered with the surplus sail at the foot folding on to or being wrapped around the boom and tied with a sail tie or long line.

> 'Your mainsail is your stability and the headsail the driving force.'

Hard on the wind and tight reaching are the best points of sailing to maintain while reefing the main. The pressure of the wind on the sail at these points will ensure that the reefed sail sets correctly and if you have to ease the mainsheet a little to make the job easier, the boom doesn't need to move very far to spill the wind. Another helpful suggestion is to ease the mainsheet after the luff edge has been reefed, to make reefing the leech easier.

Slab reefing — with this method, the sail is pulled down in slabs alongside the boom, unlike traditional points reefing in which the surplus sail is furled on top of the boom.

1   Hold course, preferably with the wind forward of the beam.
2   Let the boom vang go.
3   Remove stop/pin from the mast track.
4   Tighten the topping lift and ease out the mainsheet.
5   Ease the main halyard and pull the sail down to the boom. Hook the reef cringle on to the horn and then tighten main halyard.
6   Pull the slab reef lines at the clew and winch tight. They are usually held by a cleat or winch. If difficult to get tight, ease the mainsheet to take the load off.
7   Ease the topping lift.
8   Neaten up the surplus sail to stop it flapping, using a sail tie or lashing line through a middle cringle and around the sail (not the boom).

As a precaution against forgetting to tie in slab reefing lines, mouse lines — big, endless loops of line — can be reeved through the slab reefing cringles. If you find yourself without slab reefing lines in place, these can then be simply attached to the mouse lines with a clove hitch and pulled through the reefing cringles. Photograph shows mouse line reeved through reefing cringle and hanging down by the foot of the sail.

REEFING THE MAINSAIL

Photograph shows two slab-reefing lines permanently reeved in sail. When pulled down these cringles become the new clew for the reefed sail.

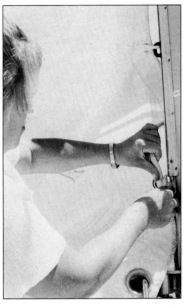

Release mainsail halyard and pull down reefing cringle over reefing horn.

Put slab reefing line onto outhaul winch for tensioning, using winch handle to tighten foot of sail. Cleat reefing line.

Tidy up surplus sail by tying lashing lines through middle cringles and around the boom. View of other side of boom shows surplus sail.

A reef in the main and sailing hard on the wind.

Extremes in reefing: folds of reefed mainsail on board a New Zealand Round-the-World Yacht Race entry 'Ceramco' in the Southern Ocean.

The problem with slab reefing is that to pull down the clew end of the main in any sort of blow or heavy sea you do have to be strong because of the pressure on the sail and weight of the boom. Most sails have a winch on the boom to assist with slab reefing. Racing yachtsmen prefer slab reefing to roller reefing because it gives them a better-shaped sail, and for the racing yacht with its crew of six or eight, slab reefing poses few problems. But if the yacht was being sailed by just two people, one would have to remain in the cockpit and handle the mainsheet while the other lowered the halyard, pulled down the tack and clew, then tightened the halyard again. To be done effectively, this would require a great deal of strength for one person.

On slab reefed sails, the lines of reef points are set at three levels up the sail, with larger holes at the respective clews and tacks through which the slab reefing lines are run. For ease of handling, these lines are often reeved permanently in the sail (it would be very difficult to reeve them during a wind of 30 knots or more). At the clew end of the boom, a reefing line is taken through a block on the boom, through a sail cringle, down and around the boom, and tied with a bowline to a saddle next to the block. Another line is taken from a secured point by the tack, up through the tack hole in the sail and back down again. I often reef the sail while still at anchor.

> Never head into the wind. Stay on course or the boom will fling around and make reefing very hard to do. Just let your mainsheet go.

the headsail

It is usually pretty obvious when you have too much headsail on: the boat leaps and pounds and will have an excessive angle of heel with the wind forward of the beam. As well, if the increasing wind has caused a seam in the headsail to pull, or if a rip has started, it's clear that the headsail should be replaced smartly before it disintegrates. A good indication with most yachts of when to change the headsail, or reef the main, is when the leeward rail is awash. If the yacht is hard to steer or handle, reduce the size of your sail.

As the headsail is the driving force of the yacht it is most important to limit the time you are without it. Without headsail control the yacht will lose steerage and jump about. It is good policy, then, especially if the yacht is short-handed, to do as much of the work of attaching the hanks of the new headsail and tying in the sheets as possible before the change is made. Two crew are usually involved with a headsail change.

1   Clip the hanks of the new sail you wish to hoist onto the forestay between the tack and first hank of the sail already up. (The tack shackle and halyard won't be changed over, of course, until the old sail is down.) Always stand on the windward side of the sail so that you can work down with gravity, rather than on the low (leeward) side and have to stretch and reach up.

2   Take out the windward sheet of the existing sail and tie it into the clew of the sail you are going to hoist.

3   Change the position of the jib sheet track slide on the windward side.

4   When all is ready, lower the jib halyard and let the leeward jib sheet go so that the old headsail can be pulled down onto the deck.

5   Quickly unhank the old headsail from the forestay.

6   Change the snap clips from the tack and head of the old sail to the tack and head of the new sail.

7   Change over the other jib sheet, tying it into the clew of the new sail with a bowline as usual. Reposition its sheet slide.

8   Hoist the new sail and trim.

9   Remove the sail you have lowered and stow quickly.

> Wedge your body in the pulpit when doing a headsail change.

Whenever you are changing headsails, you will find that the further forward in the bow you work, the easier it is to pull the sail down and get it aboard. Never head into the wind when doing a change.

In windy conditions and rough seas it is advisable to bear off your course until the wind is aft of the beam. This allows the crew to work on a flatter deck, and because the headsail is blanketed from the wind by the mainsail it is easier to lower. In bad conditions, safety harnesses should be clipped to a secure point, such as the mast, forestay, bollard or pulpit, to leave both hands free to do the job.

Headsails are usually changed in windy conditions, not reefed, but the exception is the roller furling headsail. This operates by a swivel at the top of the forestay and a drum at the bottom. The system is activated by a lazy line on the drum and may be controlled effectively from the cockpit. The line is cleated off or secured to a winch once the desired reduction in sail area is reached.

A roller-furling headsail system does away with having to carry a range of headsails and makes for a much faster headsail change. The roller-furling headsail will wear out more quickly than a conventional set of headsails — because it is left out all the time

CHANGING THE HEADSAIL

Clip hanks of new headsail onto forestay. Headsail is hanked on between tack and first hank of sail already hoisted.

Change over windward sheet from existing headsail to clew of new headsail.

Claw down the old headsail to the deck.

Unhank old sail. Change over the snap-clips to the tack and head of the new sail.

and never taken off the forestay — but you need only invest in one sail to begin with. However, sail performance, especially **on the wind** and in strong winds, is not as good as a conventional headsail hanked on. The conventional system enables a better shape to be obtained on the headsail, particularly in exerting halyard tension, and it is the headsail that is so important to sailing effectively both on the wind and in strong winds.

In good conditions you may quickly and effectively change your headsail when you go about. With this method the windward jib sheet is taken out of the sail presently hoisted and tied into the new sail, and the track slide is set before you change tacks. This makes for a faster and easier sail change in which control of the boat is not lost. As well, the old headsail will fall to the deck on going about rather than having to be clawed down.

Never stay headed directly into the wind while changing a headsail to avoid risk of injury from wildly flapping sails and sheets.

Performance of a roller-furling headsail will not be as good as with a conventional hanked headsail, but the roller-furling system enasbles a much faster sail change and does away with needing to invest in a wardrobe of headsails.

up and down the mast

If you ever have to do any work at the top of the mast, which side of the mast it is on will decide which halyard you attach the bosun's chair to. If the mast track on the aft side of the mast needs attention, then you will go up on the main halyard. If there is something to be done on the forward edge of the mast, then you will use the jib halyard.

The bosun's chair should be shackled or snap-clipped to the halyard with a sail tie also passing through the rings of the chair and the talurite just in case the snap-clip is accidentally tripped.

If you can pull yourself up as well as being winched, it will make the job an easier one for the crew on the winch. Stick your feet out in front and grab hold of the sidestays and pull yourself up.

Before you start in on the job you have been hoisted to do, make sure that the halyard is cleated off. Any tools you take up with you should be tied onto the chair with lashing lines long enough to enable the tools to be used easily.

For the ride down the mast, check first that the tools are back safely attached to the seat. Controlling a bosun's chair down the mast is best done with two turns on the winch and the crew on the winch easing the halyard with long arm motions. If this is too jerky, put on one turn only and lower slowly.

optimists and other small boats

THE PLEASURES of sailing a small centreboard yacht are very rewarding if you know the basics or if you previously enjoyed sailing a larger yacht. Things happen so much faster on a small sailing dinghy and you're often left wondering why and how they happened to you! For instance, you have to constantly duck under the boom and if you're heading into the wind instead of on your course, the boom is continually swinging from one side of the boat to the other and it can be a very dangerous situation to be in. Yacht's can't sail into the wind — you should only head into the wind when you're hoisting or lowering a sail.

wind and wave angles

A good rule of thumb when working out where the wind is coming from, is to look at any small whitecaps on the waves. The broken water on the top of the wave is the angle the wind is coming from. You can't sail head on into the white caps, but use a five-to or five-past angle from the waves or whitecaps. Larger yachts have an arrow at the top of the mast and you can easily work out where the wind is. Some smaller yachts have a wind direction arrow fitted, which are a very good idea. To work out where the wind is coming from, lay your arm pointing into the waves and say to yourself, 'Well, that is the direction where I can't sail to.' The angle that you can sail into is approximately 35° to 40° from the waves or wind. Larger yachts sail at 30° to the wind.

sailing up wind

When you want to get to where the wind is coming from, you have to move from one side of the wind to the other; this is called tacking, beating, bashing to windward, slogging or ON THE WIND. This manouvre is the only time your sails will be pulled all the way in, that is, only when the wind is at the five-to or five-past angle. To tack you zigzag from one side of the wind to the other and heel over. Use your body weight to hold the boat as flat as possible. As the wind gusts at different strengths, you can change the angle of your body weight (to keep the yacht as flat as possible). If two boats were sailing on the same course, the one sitting flatter would be going faster. Therefore, ON THE WIND is the only time you pull your sail all the way in and the boat heels over, the rest of the time it is important to ease the sails to the angle that the wind is hitting the boat. If you leave the sails in the same position, you won't move!

Every time you change course you must change the sail angle to the wind, letting it out or pulling it in. You can't just sit in the stern of the boat and expect it to sail well, you need to move your body to a central or just forward of the middle of the boat position to keep it flat or level in the water.

steering

When steering a small boat (or any boat for that matter), always use the helm (the tiller or the wheel), gently trying to avoid using full lock as the rudder acts as a brake. Small and constant movements are the key — or none at all if the sail trim is correct.

halyard tension

How tight you pull the halyard up and the outhaul out depends on how much wind there is. In light winds have light tension in your rigging, in medium winds have medium tension and in heavy, strong and puffy winds have plenty of tension on the luff (the attached edge of the sail) and pull the outhaul tight.

The kicking strap (also known as the boom vang) has its most important role when the wind is aft of the beam, as it holds the boom flat when you ease the mainsheet out. The further aft the wind comes the tighter the kicking strap should be. The kicking strap is not so important when sailing to windward, it is important when the wind is past the 50° angle.

The mainsheet is a small yacht's accelerator. It controls the leach tension, which adds to your power. I recommend constant movement, trimming in and out of the mainsheet just a little when you are sailing on the wind; it is quite easy to stall or jam your boat speed if you have the mainsheet hard in.

tacking

When moving upwind it is always difficult to work out how often to tack. You need to consider how much wind there is. Tacking in a strong puff is always advisable as each time you tack you will lose about three boat lengths. Carefully consider the proximity of other boats, if you misjudge you may have to dip under their stern. Always try to go around the other boat's stern and not its bow, especially if your are at close quarters and on the port tack.

port and starboard (see page 90 for illustration)

If the wind is on your port side you are on the port tack and must give way to all other sailing boats. If two boats are on the port tack, the windward yacht will give way to the leward yacht. When you are on the starboard tack, you have the wind on your starboard side and you have the right of way over other yachts. A windward yacht will give way to a leward yacht if you are both on the same tack.

in irons

If you are stuck in irons, that is heading into the wind with the wind funelling down both sides of your sail, keep your head down and hold the tiller hard over to one side, keeping the mainsheet all the way in. You will move backwards, but stay in the same position and you will move out of 'in irons' and end up on the port or starboard tack. You end up in irons because you have been trying to sail too close to the wind or have experienced a wind change that has caused you to head into the wind.

turning the boat

There are only two ways to turn your boat; either by GOING ABOUT into the wind or by GYBING, moving away from the wind and turning the boat towards the boom. Going about is slower than gybing. If the wind is forward of the beam you should go about, if it is aft of the beam you should gybe. If you decide to gybe remember it is going to be fast and your boom will swing violently if it is windy. Say to yourself 'a-bout, a-bout, a-bow into the wind' to remind yourself which way you are going to turn the boat.

When gybing make sure the centreboard is down so the vang and sheet can not get caught on it. Be prepared to move your bodyweight very quickly to counteract the weight of the wind in the sail when it changes from one side to the other. A simple rule to remember is that upwind you should go about, and downwind you should gybe.

The centreboard should be all the way down going upwind and up a little if you dare going downwind. Make sure you are feeling confident about your position before you try lifting the board up a bit when the sails are eased.

capsizing

The sooner you capsize your small boat the better, as once done you will not have to worry about it. If the yacht capsizes, either go over the hull to the centreboard, or if you fall in the water swim around, climb onto the centreboard and haul yourself into the boat. Bail out the water as soon as possible.

setting your sails

The further forward that to winds come across your boat the further in the sails will be and when the wind comes aft the sails go out. If the wind hits you on your beam at the halfway mark of your boat the sails go out halfway.

With the wind hitting your boat at five-to or five-past, the sail will be all the way in. If the wind hits your boat at ten-to or ten-past, the sails will be one-third of the way out. If wind is on the beam, your sails will be halfway out. When it hits your boat at 20-to or 20 past, the sails will be two-thrids of the way out. Only when the wind is coming over your stern will your sails be all the way out. At this point, remember that this is when your are likely to experience an uncontrolled gybe and you are at a roly point of sailing.

Have fun, keep a smile on your face and each time you go out you will improve. Most importantly, don't forget that the basics of sailing are the same on any sized yacht. Children learn best on small sailing dinghies, however, adults tend to find it much easier to learn to sail in a larger vessel, then applying what they have learnt to SAILING SMALLER YACHTS.

safety at sea

When it's cold but not wet, a jacket like this is ideal to provide warmth without affecting your movement around the boat. Jacket should be long enough to maintain warmth and protection over base of your back when you bend — a lot of jackets can be too short to do so. Warm lining is synthetic, much more practical aboard than wool, which is difficult to dry thoroughly and which smells when damp. With a synthetic lining like this jacket's, all you need is to give the jacket a bit of a shake when you hang it up and very soon it's as good as dry.

CAREFUL PLANNING will prevent many potential accidents at sea. In an unavoidable accident it may mean the difference between coping and not.

Every person sailing with you should have their own wet-weather clothing, safety harness, and lifejacket or buoyancy vest. They should also be aware of, and be able to handle, the emergencies that may arise — from being caught in heavy weather, to man overboard or fire. Crew should know where safety equipment is stowed and how to use it.

At sea, help from other agencies is further away than it is on land — often a lot further away — and all crew, especially wives and families, need to be self-sufficient in their knowledge and use of emergency aids.

The boat should be equipped with a life raft if going offshore, otherwise a rubber dinghy or wooden dinghy with built-in buoyancy capable of holding all the crew, and you must always carry flares. Also, depending on the type of sailing you are doing, your boat should have spare lifebelts, a dan buoy, emergency beacon, transceiver radio, fire extinguishers, radar reflector, medical kit, tools, and sufficient spares to repair and replace damaged rigging and fittings.

The best precaution against avoidable accidents and injuries aboard is, of course, prevention. Get into the habit of regularly checking rigging, fittings, sails and fuel, and electrical, water and gas systems. Now and then rehearse with all the crew the action that should be taken in emergency situations. Know the changing weather, sea conditions and tides that may necessitate altering course, changing the headsail, or reefing the main.

clothing

You must have clothing that will keep you warm and dry in the worst of the cold and wet that can arise at sea. A bad weather kit should include a warm hat, gloves, waterproof parka and leggings, socks, warm sweater and trousers. Keep in mind that most body heat is lost through the extremities (feet, hands and head), and ensure these

A warm vest is great for when it's not cold enough to need a full jacket. Material is pliable and soft and will withstand years of hard use.

If it's wet and cold, then wet-weather gear is necessary. A jacket alone will still leave you with a cold wet backside and legs. Wrists and pockets have Velcro fasteners for quick closing.

areas are particularly well protected.

Woollen garments take longer to become saturated than synthetics, but they also take longer to dry. All in all, synthetic clothing is more convenient and useful aboard. Under most conditions sandshoes or running-type shoes are suitable for getting around on deck. 'Lil grippers' are great if it is wet or cold.

safety harness

Ideally there should be a safety harness for each member of the crew, including all children aboard, each harness properly adjusted for the individual. When sailing short-handed or in strong winds it is wise to put on a harness and to wear it when going forward to do a job. This leaves you both hands free to get on with your job.

Rather than clipping yourself on and off from the stanchions — which limits you to a radius of about 1 to 1.5 metres, the usual length of the lanyard clipped to the harness — it is a good idea to reeve two lines each side between backstay and forestay to which the harness lanyard can be attached, so that you are operating on a

'Lil grippers'.

Worries over children aboard are considerably reduced if they are given a harness to wear.

Attach harness lanyard to safety harness by passing lanyard eye through harness rings then threading other end through the eye. Pull lanyard tight to bring harness rings together.

running line. Ensure that you can clip on from near the hatchway before going on deck.

Wearing a harness enables you to get on with the job — at the mast or the bow, or whenever you need both hands — without having to give part of your concentration. In a particularly heavy sea, the helmsman may find wearing two harnesses fixed at advantageous points makes it easier to stand up while the boat is being tossed about.

Harnesses can be kept in a locker near the hatchway, where they will be readily available to crew going out on deck, or in the pocket of your wet-weather suit. The harness lanyard should be long enough to allow freedom of movement, but never so long that you could go overboard leeward while clipped to the windward line.

Generally children are far better off in a safety harness than a bulky lifejacket, which restricts movement and makes it difficult for them to build up confidence while sailing. In really bad conditions children should wear both a lifejacket and safety harness, or be made to stay below clipped into their bunks with the lee cloths up.

My children never came aboard our boat without their harnesses on. My son Carl was walking around the deck in a harness at 10 months. When we left home he'd put his harness on, and then at the boat he'd just clip himself to the line on deck. If he went below, he clipped himself to the line in the cabin or into a bunk. He never walked around the boat without his harness; it became a habit with him never having known anything different.

I didn't make him wear a lifejacket aboard the yacht, only a harness, but when going in the dinghy he wore a lifejacket. I make toddlers wear their harnesses backwards so that the lanyard trails off

Lifebelts should be stowed handy to the cockpit from where they can be thrown if a person falls overboard. A lifebelt forward of the wheel means that the helmsman can reach it without having to leave off steering.

behind them, making it easier for them to potter about on deck. The lanyards on children's harnesses will need to be adjusted as the children grow.

lifejackets and buoyancy vests

This is a matter of personal choice. Ninety-nine per cent of the time a buoyancy vest will be a lot more convenient and less restrictive to wear on deck. If you fell in the water, it would provide all the flotation you needed. A lifejacket is much more bulky and anyone wearing one on deck for any length of time is going to be a liability. While a lifejacket will keep an unconscious person's face out of the water, I have my doubts about its general practicality. However, there must be a lifejacket for every person aboard.

Boats should carry a range of flares, including smoke, handheld and parachute types. A large plastic container with sealing top is essential if flares are to be kept dry.

flares

The types and numbers of flares you should carry depend upon the kind of sailing you're doing, but even small-boat inshore sailors should carry them. They really will draw attention to your plight and help pinpoint your position if you get into a fix. There is a variety of hand-held, buoyant and rocket flares, and the minimum you should have is a couple of white or orange smoke signals for daytime use, a couple of red hand flares for poor-visibility, daytime use or at night, and a rocket flare.

One manufacturer produces a pack of miniflares that comes with a small gun to fire them. There are a number of shots in a pack so you have more chance of being seen. The whole thing comes in a sealed plastic packet that can be kept in your jacket pocket.

Rocket flares turn into the wind and should always be fired a few degrees off to leeward. Always hold hand flares downwind to prevent them dropping burning material over you. Different kinds of flares are activated in different ways, so familiarise yourself with them before you need to use them. Always check expiry dates on your flares and replace them before they become outdated.

life raft

The life raft should be able to accommodate all the people aboard. It should be stowed on deck just aft of the mast, or in a deck locker where it is accessible in an emergency. If you had to use the life raft, it would be thrown overboard to leeward, in its (most commonly) rigid fibreglass case with its painter securely tied to a strong point on the boat. Pulling on the painter trips the gas bottle, which inflates the raft. Once it is inflated you pull it alongside, get in, and then cut the painter. A knife should be kept in a holder handy to the mast area and there should be one in the cockpit also.

Most life rafts are covered with a self-erecting canopy and come complete with flares, food and water, and survival gear such as fishing lines and bailers. However, you may like to make up your own additional emergency pack that could be slung aboard the life raft should you have to get into it.

A life raft costs several thousand dollars and every care should be taken to see it is properly maintained and inspected by the manufacturers once a year. Most rafts are of rubber-fabric construction and quickly perish if exposed to sun and salt water. Salt water penetrating the seal at the case joint dries to leave salt crystals

A cover protects life raft from salt spray and sunlight. Not visible in this picture is a knife kept in a pocket in the cover, where it is handy for cutting away lashings holding the life raft in place.

Most life rafts are canopied to provide shelter from sun and rain.

that cause abrasive action on the rubber. Ensure the joint is well sealed. If stowing the raft on deck, keep a cover over the case to shed the worst of the salt spray that comes over the deck.

If there is no deck locker, tie the life raft on the cabin top. Boats rarely sink so fast that you wouldn't be able to go forward to get it in an emergency. Don't allow anyone to sit or stand on the life raft while stowed on deck in case it is damaged.

dan buoy

Also known as the Danford marker buoy, this piece of safety equipment is usually carried only on long passages. It is generally attached up the backstay or tied along the lifelines and is used in the event of a man overboard in heavy seas, or at night. The 3 to 3.6 metre-long dan buoy pole is thrown overboard to mark the man-overboard position. Attached to it are a life ring, whistle, dye marker and flashing white light. The pole is weighted at the bottom to keep it upright, and a float about a third to halfway up keeps the top of the pole above the waves. At the top of the pole is a brightly coloured flag.

fire extinguishers

As with life rafts, ensure that extinguishers are kept where you can get them easily, that every crew member knows how to use them, and that they are regularly serviced. Carbon dioxide and dry powder extinguishers should be used on all electrical, fuel and galley fires; never use water. Select extinguishers that have the capacity you need and are simple to operate.

first aid

Make sure there is a fully stocked first aid kit complete with manual. All the medical emergencies — including heart attack and toothache — that happen on land can also occur while at sea, plus some, so be prepared to deal with them.

It's not a bad idea for each crew member to bring his or her own medical kit of particular items they know they could need.

safety on deck

A casual approach to sailing can lead to injury or worse. Always remember you are on a moving deck with the ocean all around, and hold onto something with at least one hand when moving about the deck.

* Non-slip material should be affixed to the tread areas of the deck and cabin roof; continually remove loose items from the deck so they won't be tripped over.

* Respect flapping sheets and swinging booms; both can inflict severe injury on the unwary.

* Always walk along the windward side of the boat, not the leeward. The angle of the windward deck is a more comfortable one to be on, and if you fall you will fall only onto the deck. If you fell on the leeward side, you could go overboard. When you are on the windward side of a boat you are on top of the problem, it's not on top of you.

survival in the water

If you fall overboard and the boat does not immediately gybe to pick you up, kick off your footwear and attempt to get out of any heavy outer clothing, especially wet–weather gear and long pants. Footwear and outer clothing can become heavy in the water and weigh you down. If you have to, take a big breath and go under in order to strip off your pants — you will be a lot more buoyant without them.

Once you have got rid of your outer clothing, don't panic, but instead just rest on your back, kicking your feet and sculling your hands to help you stay afloat. If you are wearing a buoyancy aid to which is attached a whistle, blow this at regular intervals to guide the boat back to you.

If the yacht has gybed, it is impossible for you to be run over as it will be heading into the wind and slowing all the time. If the man overboard gybe manoeuvre (see following) has been carried out immediately, the boat should be back alongside you in about 30 or 40 seconds.

man overboard

JUST GYBE AND LET THE SHEETS GO!

As soon as someone has gone overboard the aim is to stop the boat in its tracks and get back to that person. The best and quickest way to do this is to gybe immediately and let all the sheets go when they collapse (normal time you let sheet go). No matter what point you're sailing on, no matter what the conditions are like, no matter what part of the boat the person has gone over — if someone's life is in danger, then gybe and let all the sheets go. You'll go round quickly and stop back alongside the person in the water. Hold helm hard over to complete the circle.

Man overboard drill: over goes the polystyrene marker.

2 seconds: the boat is turned into a gybe and the sheets let go.

25 seconds: gybed and heading into the wind, slowing as it approaches the marker.

30 seconds: the bow alongside marker. Elapsed time would have been shorter in a stronger wind.

The boat will nearly always turn within its waterline length. You then straighten up as you approach the person in the water and try to get them onto leeward. Where this procedure is put into action immediately after the person has gone overboard, it is possible to be back with them in about 30 to 40 seconds.

Much has been written on the subject of rescuing a person who has gone overboard, most of it describing a lengthy and risky procedure in which the boat continues away from the man overboard for up to half a minute, then goes about, sails back to the position on a reciprocal course, and finally rounds up alongside. Depending upon the skipper, this could take up to several minutes! Now, the visible portion of someone who has fallen into the water is immediately reduced to their head and perhaps a waving arm, which very quickly gets smaller as the boat pulls away. And that's in broad daylight in a moderate sea. Imagine the difficulty in keeping a sight on a man overboard and returning to him or her in heavy weather and/or at night.

If you were on a broad reach in a lot of wind, say over 35 knots, it's possible when you gybe to rip the sail, break the boom, even the mast. It's unlikely, however, and even that must weigh lightly against the greater chance gybing has of saving someone's life. Such damage won't sink the boat and you will be able to repair it. In addition, going about means returning with the wind in your sails and under speed, which puts the man overboard at risk.

If you are sailing short-handed, don't bother attempting to throw out lifelines or lifebuoys; just get the boat around as fast as possible, and that can only be achieved by gybing it — turning the boat towards the main boom. If there are plenty of people aboard, someone else could throw out a lifebuoy, but if you're at the helm and there's no-one close by, forget it and simply gybe. As you do so you can lean forward, uncleat the mainsheet and let it go as the mainsail collapses; similarly with the jib — uncleat the jib sheet and let it go when it collapses. The boat will spin around, head to the wind, and slow to a stop near the person in the water.

The point cannot be repeated too often: under no circumstances go about if somebody's life is in danger. Not only will it take longer, but there's a good chance you'll run down the person in the water.

Several tragic deaths have occurred when the person in the water was run down by the boat they fell off. This cannot happen if you gybe.

If a man is overboard, do not drop the sails, start the motor, get in the water with them, or panic. None of these will do any good. It

Bowline is passed over the head of the person in the water and under their arms. Free end of bowline goes over end of boom and on to winch.

is much better to stay on deck and to gybe the boat and get it back alongside them. Tempting as it might be to go in after someone, particularly your own child, resist it and instead get the boat back immediately to him or her. If you go in as well, there are two people to haul out. Thrashing about in the water trying to save your child will probably only raise the child's panic.

Once alongside the person in the water, it becomes a matter of getting them aboard again. If they are conscious and young and strong it should be easy enough to get them up a stern ladder or on a rope over one of the aft sides. However, if they are unconscious or elderly, or large and heavy, you will have to get a rope around them. Tie a bowline with a big loop in it and having brought them alongside with the boathook, pass the loop over their head and then get it around their chest under their arms. Throw the free end of the bowline over the boom, then take it around a winch. Winch the person up out of the water and pull them aboard.

If short-handed, cleat off the rope after winching the person out of the water, swing the boom in, and ease the person down into the cockpit. It is the easiest thing in the world if you use the leverage provided by the boom and winch.

If you do have to get into the water, then tie a bowline around yourself and tie it tightly to a secure point on the boat (not to a lifeline or stanchion).

forecasting the weather

MORE THAN ANY other factor, your safety at sea depends on the prevailing weather and tide conditions. Many accidents that occur at sea can be prevented if those concerned, before setting out, spend a few minutes checking the existing weather and sea conditions. Check the weather conditions before you go out and monitor the weather constantly while at sea. If the forecast is bad, stay at home; if you are already at sea and the weather deteriorates, find shelter or return home. If you decide to return home, never underestimate how quickly the weather can deteriorate -- even in apparently fine weather, storms and squalls can arise, so at the first sign of threatening weather seek shelter. Above all, know the limits of your experience and the capabilities of your craft.

marine forecasts

Before setting out you should check the marine forecasts for your area. It is important to obtain marine forecasts since forecasts for land areas are generally not applicable to sea conditions.

A great deal of weather forecast information is available to sailors to provide them with a knowledge of future weather conditions and to update the situation day-by-day. Newspapers, radio and television all provide weather information and special marine forecasts can be heard on national and local radio stations. If you have a radio-telephone, forecasts are also broadcast on regional R/T services. More information is available from your local meteorological office and coastguard.

Bear in mind that any forecast may be at odds with the actual situation and that local features may affect the weather you are receiving: keep a weather eye out.

One of the most important indicators of weather conditions is the wind speed. In forecasts, wind speeds are calculated as the mean or average speed over several minutes. However, winds can be expected to exceed the mean speed by as much as 50 per cent, and in very gusty conditions close to headlands or steep terrain winds can increase to twice the mean speed forecast.

Marine forecasts also give an indication of visibility and

likelihood of showers or rain.

Swell conditions are also given, with a prediction of swell height and direction.

predicting the weather

Because forecasts can cover a vast area, their overview of weather conditions is never comprehensive, and may even be at odds with what is actually happening. Never take the marine forecasts as gospel and instead learn to predict the weather patterns for yourself. Squalls and storms can occur suddenly and unless you are aware of the warning signs, your life can be in danger. In particular watch out for these conditions:

* Cirrus clouds: High, delicately defined clouds that appear as strands, patches or as a thin sheet. These are a characteristic feature of depressions which form north of New Zealand. Expect a change for the worse usually within 24 to 48 hours.
* Cumulus clouds: These clouds with their familiar cotton-wool shape are a sign of unstable conditions. Expect wind gusts.
* Cumulonimbus clouds: These large towering clouds building high in the sky are a sign of thunderstorms. Beware. Although there might be gentle, steady winds blowing towards the storm clouds, severe and sudden squalls may strike.
* Fast-moving low clouds: The appearance of these clouds precedes a sharp increase in wind speed.
* Wind change: Any wind change, especially when cumulus and cumulonimbus clouds are present, is a warning that squalls or gusts are about to strike.

tides

Never under-estimate the effect that wind and tides can have on local sea conditions, especially in harbours and shallow coastal areas. When the tide is running in the same direction as the wind, sea conditions will often be smooth, but when the tide changes, the sea can become choppy and the conditions rough. As well, weather conditions, particularly in summer, can change on the tide.

Before going out always check the tide and wind direction. A pleasant afternoon's outing can quickly turn into a life-endangering encounter in rough seas. Take a copy of the tide tables with you.

Learning to interpret cloud formations assists the skipper in predicting future weather. These stratocumulus mean overcast conditions but probably clearing with rain unlikely.

rules of the road

'Red-to-red, green to green, entering a harbour or waterway; opposite leaving.

FAMILIARITY WITH THE basic regulations for preventing collisions at sea is an important part of sailing. Whether you are sailing or motoring out of a marina or up an estuary, you are governed by a set of nautical rules of the road. Every person responsible for a boat should know their obligations when there is a risk of collision. These rules can be summarised as follows:

port and starboard

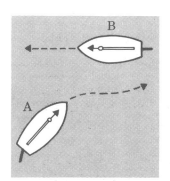

Two power-driven vessels crossing: boat A sees boat B to starboard and keeps clear.

To remember the nautical terms for the left and right of a boat (as you look forward) and their respective coloured flags or navigational lights, try these simple memory aids:

STARBOARD is RIGHT and GREEN — all longer words than PORT is LEFT is RED. As well: 'The RED ship LEFT PORT'.

Two boats sailing on opposite tacks — the boat on the starboard tack (that is, with the wind coming over the starboard side) has right of way over the boat on port tack.

Two boats sailing on the same tack — the boat to leeward has right of way over the windward boat.

Overtaking — an overtaking vessel must keep clear of all other craft.

Sail meeting power-driven — in most circumstances a boat under sail has right of way over a power-driven vessel . . . but not always. When the power-driven boat is fishing, for example, or restricted in its ability to manoeuvre, the boat under sail must keep clear and avoid collision. Also, ferries, ships, and vessels towing have right of way.

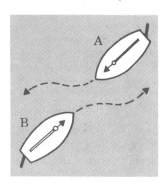

Two power-driven vessels meeting head-on: both alter course to starboard and always pass port-to-port.

If you are on a port tack you should be continually aware of giving way when necessary to all other sailing vessels. If on a starboard tack you can relax more, although you obviously still have to keep a lookout. For instance, some windsurfers have dubious control over their craft and can suddenly fall off in your path, and right of way then becomes a secondary consideration to avoiding an accident.

Two power-driven boats meeting — if meeting head-on, or nearly so, both must alter course to starboard so they pass port to port.

Two power-driven boats crossing — the boat that has the other on its starboard side keeps clear or gives way.

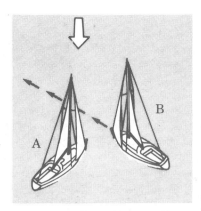

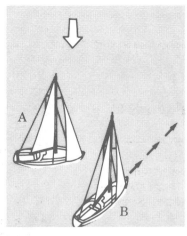

**Two boats sailing on opposite tacks:
Boat A on port tack keeps clear of boat
B on starboard tack.**

**Two boats on the same tack: Windward
boat A keeps clear of leeward boat B.**

In narrow channels — especially those in marinas — boats under
motor must keep to the starboard side of the fairway.

When you have the wind coming over the starboard side, you are
on a starboard tack and have right of way over other sailing vessels.

1   A boat under sail is one that is being propelled only by the
     wind. If the boat's motor is also going, then the boat is
     defined as power-driven.
2   If the risk of collision exists, the boat that should give way
     should do so in good time and in a way that is clear to the
     other vessel. The boat that has the right of way should keep
     its course and speed unless a collision appears likely.
3   As an aid to remembering the first rule: STARBOARD is your
     RIGHT, you are in the RIGHT; PORT is RED is DANGER, be
     prepared to GIVE WAY.

The risk of collision with another approaching boat can be
determined by considering its relative angle of bearing. Sight the
other boat against a point on your boat — such as the mast, the
winch or a point on the rail — or against any land behind the other
boat. Watch its progress in relation to that point without changing
your course or the position from which you are sighting. If the other
boat moves steadily forward on your point of reference, then you will
pass safely behind. If the boat drops aft of the point of reference,
then you will pass in front of it. If the other boat maintains its
position against your reference point, then you are on a collision
course and should take evasive action.

In this photograph, the righthand boat of the pair is to leeward and so has the right of way over the other.

daymarks and lights

All skippers of sailing craft must realise their obligations in displaying lights and shapes, both while under sail and while under power. Lights must be displayed from sunset to sunrise by all craft not at anchor, made fast to the shore or underground. Whenever being driven by its engine — whether or not its sails are set — a sailing boat is defined as a power-driven vessel within the meaning of the rules.

A boat at anchor must display one black ball forward, where best seen. Small boats of less than 7 metres need not show anchor lights or shapes when at anchor away from other shipping.

A boat under power with sails set (motorsailing) must display one black cone, point down, forward where best seen.

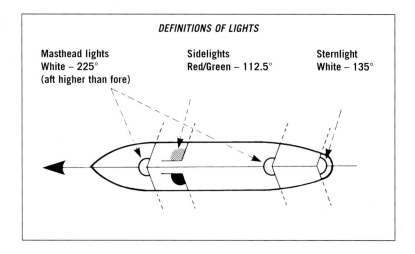

DEFINITIONS OF LIGHTS

Masthead lights
White – 225°
(aft higher than fore)

Sidelights
Red/Green – 112.5°

Sternlight
White – 135°

RECOGNITION OF LIGHTS

Optional

Optional

AHEAD

Optional

ASTERN

◀ A sailing vessel underway (not using power) and less than 20 metres length must show sidelights separate or combined, and sternlight — with optional addition of all-round red over green at top of mast or sidelights and sternlight combined in one light at the top of the mast ('tricolour light').

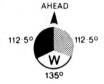

AHEAD

112·5°   112·5°

W

135°

For a power-driven vessel underway:
Less than 20 metres in length — lights must include a masthead light, sidelights and sternlight; sidelights may be a combined lantern mounted on the fore/aft centre-line of the vessel.

◀ *Less than 12 metres in length* — masthead light, sidelights and sternlight, or an all-round masthead light and sidelights (no sternlight).

Less than 7 metres in length — and whose maximum speed does not exceed 7 knots: vessels may, instead of the above lights, exhibit an all-round white light. Sidelights shall also be shown if practicable.

A boat at anchor must display one black ball forward, where best seen. Small boats of less than 7 metres need not show anchor lights or shapes when at anchor away from other shipping.

▲ A sailing vessel underway (not using power) and less than 7 metres length, and boats under oars should show if practicable any of the combination of sailing boats underway. Or an electric torch or lighted lantern showing a white light and exhibited in sufficient time to prevent collision.

chapter 12

chartwork and navigation

TO SAIL YOUR BOAT from place to place in safety you must be able to determine your position, how to get to where you want to go, and how to get back again. This depends — in the case of day and weekend trips — upon the study of charts, the use of a compass and the ability to relate the two.

It is not enough to expect that you are always going to be within sight of land and will always be able to see where you are. I have been on numerous day and weekend trips when all sight of land has been lost due to heavy rain and squalls and it is then that you are glad of the record you've kept of course steered, time and last known position.

It is easy to keep such a record and it adds another dimension to even the shortest trip. It can be fun as well as useful to plot efficient courses and to estimate the time of arrival at your destination.

It is my belief that in chartwork for the great majority of sailing you will do — that is, weekend or holiday coastal cruising — there is absolutely no need ever to plot courses and bearings in anything but magnetic north. The boat's compass points to magnetic north and you will be steering your course by the compass so do all your chartwork in magnetic as well as using the middle magnetic compass rose. Forget all about true north on your local chart. If the magnetic rose is printed, use it.

At the same time you can forget about annual increase in variation. If you purchase the most up-to-date chart available, annual increase will have been adjusted up to the time of publication. Then, with the annual local rate of increase of about 4 minutes, by the time it finally amounts to anything approaching a degree (60'), the chart will be so old and well-thumbed that it will need replacing by a new updated one in which someone else has worked out all the maths and made the adjustments.

As for deviation, its effect in most instances is very slight in relation to your ability to steer a course. For most skippers the quality of their course, after all the business of adjusting true course for change in variation and deviation, just won't be worth the effort.

'MM, middle magnetic.'

The compass should be mounted where the helmsman can readily refer to it.

Steering compass.

the compass

The magnetised needle of a compass points to magnetic north and a compass is used to take magnetic bearings in order that we can fix our position, and to steer a course that we have plotted on a chart.

Your steering compass should be clearly marked in degrees from 0° to 360° and mounted in gimbals so that the bowl and card stay level no matter what the heel on the boat. As well, the compass should have built-in lighting.

Most steering compasses have a line across their bowls called the lubberline. The compass is mounted so that this line is set directly in line with the bow of the boat. When you are using the compass to steer a magnetic course you bring the boat around until the desired course (for example 060°M.) is under the lubberline. You keep it there to maintain your course, or as near as you can to it. Most newcomers to sailing find it difficult to steer within 4° to 5° of a course, but with practice you should be able to keep within 3°. At first, forget about magnetic courses and instead simply teach yourself to steer a straight course on a landmark.

To use hand-bearing compass, hold horizontal and sight landmark across the top of the sights.

When not in use, the compass should be kept covered and out of the sun.

While the steering compass is fine for steering a course by, it is difficult to use for taking a bearing of a land object in order to fix your position without actually turning the boat around to point directly at the object. For taking bearings you need a hand-bearing compass. This is held horizontally, and the land object sighted across the sights while the bearing is read through the prism.

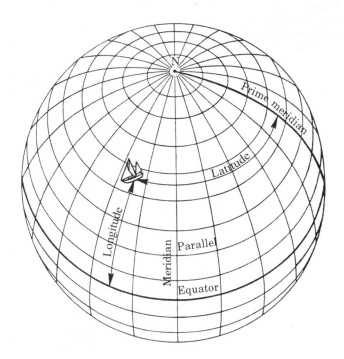

Position expressed in terms of latitude and longitude. Latitude is distance and are the lines that run sideways around the globe. Longitude equals time zones and are the lines that run up and down the globe.

charts

'Latitude is distance, longitude is time zones, the long lines up and down the globe. Remember the difference by remembering 'a long, long time'.

The position of any object on the earth's surface can be expressed in terms of latitude, the lines running east-west around the earth, and longitude, the lines running north-south over the poles. The first is measured in degrees, minutes and points of a minute of an arc north or south of the equator; the second is measured similarly but of an arc east or west of the Greenwich meridian.

The Greenwich meridian is almost universally regarded today as the prime meridian from which longitude is reckoned, but this wasn't always the case. In the past there were a number of different meridians used, varying from country to country, but the Greenwich meridian was adopted in the 1840s following its popularisation by British map-makers in the late 1700s.

So longitude came to be reckoned from the Greenwich meridian and with it a common system of reckoning local time. Countries around the globe base their time on meridians usually a whole number of hours from Greenwich in a system called the time zone system. East of Greenwich, hours are subtracted from local time. Westwards, hours are added until the change of day at the

This reproduction of a section of a chart for the Bay of Islands shows the compass rose that is printed on some New Zealand charts. The compass rose on each chart shows the magnetic variation applicable to the particular area, in this case 17° 58'E. The middle ring is the magnetic direction — middle magnetic (MM) — and is the one to use for plotting courses and bearings.

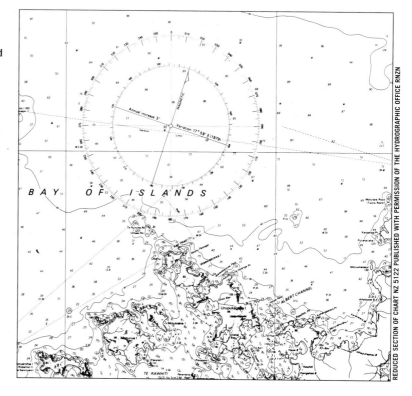

REDUCED SECTION OF CHART NZ 5122 PUBLISHED WITH PERMISSION OF THE HYDROGRAPHIC OFFICE RNZN

1	Gd	Ground
2	S	Sand
3	M	Mud
4	Oz	Ooze
8	Sn	Shingle
10	St	Stones
11	R	Rocks
11a	Bo	Boulders
24	Oy	Oysters
25	Ms	Mussels
26	Sp	Sponge
28	Wd	Weed
(Sc)	SM/R	Layered bottom (sand & mud over rock)

PUBLISHED WITH PERMISSION OF THE HYDROGRAPHIC OFFICE RNZN

Selection of chart abbreviations relating to the quality of the sea floor, and their meanings.

international date line. New Zealand, for example, keeps time in winter (summer daylight saving complicates matters slightly during the months it is in operation) on a meridian of 180° east of Greenwich and is exactly 12 hours ahead of Greenwich. On the other hand, the East Coast of the United States calculates time on a meridian of 75°W, five hours behind Greenwich.

By determining our position relative to both latitude and longitude, we can then relate it to a map or chart of the world.

Always use the largest-scale charts available. Not only will they provide you with greater detail, but also any errors you make in plotting will mean less error in your actual position. As well, your charts should be the most up-to-date ones available in order that they provide the latest information and corrections.

Local charts all carry two printed compass roses or circles marked off into 360°. The outer circle shows true north — the direction to which the chart is orientated, north-south running on the perpendicular — and the inner circle magnetic north (M). Information on magnetic variation (see following) is printed across the middle of the two roses.

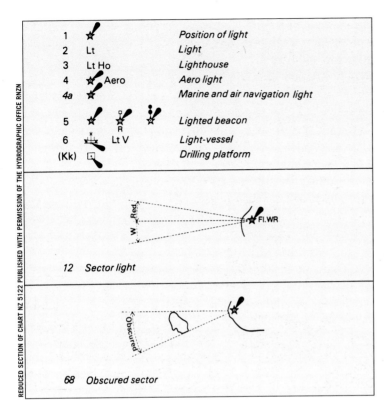

REDUCED SECTION OF CHART NZ 5122 PUBLISHED WITH PERMISSION OF THE HYDROGRAPHIC OFFICE RNZN

Light symbols commonly seen on charts.

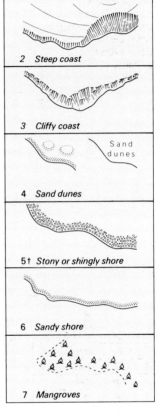

Selection of coastline features and their meanings.

These, which must be learnt, are the four most important chart symbols.

Degrees and minutes of a degree of latitude are printed down the sides of charts, and degrees and minutes of a degree of longitude along the top and bottom.

When buying your first charts, also purchase a copy of the Chart Catalogue and Index, which explains all of the symbols and abbreviations found on New Zealand charts. Study this publication so that you can readily identify the marks and the coding. Charts and the Chart Catalogue and Index can be bought at a hydrographic office and most ships' chandlers.

When plotting a course on your chart, always use a soft pencil, so that mistakes and previous courses can be easily removed. Always lay the dividers across the chart when measuring, and do not stand them straight up and down, which forces the sharp ends of the dividers into the chart and damages it.

Internationally, charts are gradually being converted — as charts are reprinted — from the old imperial measures to metrics. However, this is limited to vertical distance (depth of water, height of landmarks, etc.) only, and not horizontal distance. The nautical sea mile will not be changed. It relates to latitude, being equal to 1 minute of latitude, and is not affected by this change. Read the information on your charts carefully to determine whether they are in imperial or metric.

Charts are best kept folded in half and flat rather than rolled.

variation

Owing to its construction, a magnetic compass points to magnetic north pole and not to the earth's true, geographical north pole. The difference between these two poles is called magnetic variation and varies depending upon where you are on the earth's surface. As already mentioned, the compass rose on a chart also provides information on local variation and whether it is east of true north or west of it. A chart of the Bay of Islands area, for example, will show that local variation there is approximately 18°E, while one for the Marlborough Sounds shows a variation of 20°E.

Magnetic bearings are converted to true north bearings by adding easterly variation and subtracting westerly variation.

Variation for the whole of New Zealand is east of true north, so in New Zealand when converting any true bearings to magnetic north, you subtract variation.

The earth's magnetic field is constantly changing and the poles constantly moving. This rate of change in the position of magnetic north relative to New Zealand is about 3° each year, an increase so negligible that if you are using a reasonably up-to-date chart, you can entirely forget about it. (You can understand how really insignificant this increase is when you consider that very few people can steer within 3° of their course: there are 60' to a degree and here we are talking about just 3°!)

Having discussed the difference between true north and magnetic north and how courses can be converted from one to the other, I am now going to say — for the vast majority of sailing you are likely to do so anyway — 'Forget all about true north'. Your compass points to magnetic north, you will always steer to a magnetic course, the inner compass rose on any chart orientates it to magnetic north. There is absolutely no need — for the purposes of weekend or Christmas cruising — to ever consider true north. It can only be confusing. Forget all about it. I would even suggest you take a pencil and scribble over the outside true north compass rose to remind you not to use it. Concentrate instead on middle magnetic.

Of course if you were considering a long ocean passage you would be using charts orientated to true north. In which case you would need to know how to convert true north bearings to a magnetic course you could steer by, and to have done celestial navigation. But for weekend cruising, forget all about true north, and forget all about variation. It's worthwhile knowing what they are but don't bother about the maths, deal solely with magnetic north.

I find a good little rhyme is:

Anything west,

Compass is best.

Anything east,

Compass is least.

deviation

Because of the attracting forces of magnets, and iron and steel within the boat — such as the keel, anchor, fuel tank — the compass reading of north may differ from both true and magnetic north. This magnetic interference is called deviation, and will differ from boat to boat, being less in a fibreglass craft and greater in steel and concrete boats, which contain more metal.

Modern compasses, constructed using materials less susceptible to interference and suspended in fluid, do not have deviations as great as those of compasses made 50 or 60 years ago. If your

A deviation card should be kept near the steering compass. Each card is unique for the compass it applies to, and only while that compass remains in the position it was adjusted for.

Diagram illustrates the difference between magnetic, true and compass north, and the effects of variation and deviation.

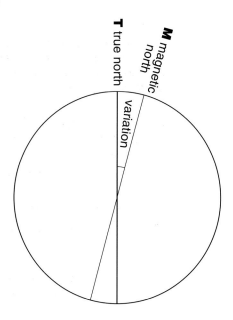

compass has a deviation of just 1° or 2°, it hardly matters for all practical purposes, but a larger deviation should be recorded and its effect on steering a course taken into account.

Unlike variation, deviation changes as the boat's direction changes. The amount of deviation shown by the compass on your boat can be calculated by a skilled compass adjuster. A deviation card will be filled out to show the effect on the compass when the boat is on various headings.

Deviation is either east or west of magnetic north. When the compass is deviated east of magnetic north, subtract the deviation to the magnetic bearing on the chart to obtain the correct bearing. When deviation is west of magnetic north, add the deviation.

In order to reduce the effects of magnetic interference on your compass, position it as far away as possible from switches and instruments and large metal fixtures and fittings — even winches can have an effect. As well, the higher above the deck the compass can be set, the further it will be away from the metal engine, keel and — in the case of a steel yacht — the hull. Should your deviation be less than 3°, it can be ignored for all of the more basic chartwork.

plotting equipment

Parallel rules — these are constructed so that the two halves are able to keep the same angle while they are stepped or rolled across the surface of the chart. A line on the chart representing the track you want to take is transferred using the rules to the middle dot of the compass rose and there converted to a course to steer. Conversely, a course can be transferred from the compass rose to anywhere on the chart using the parallel rules.

Dividers — a pair of pointed dividers (preferably of brass for robustness and long life) is used to measure distances on the chart.

Pencil and eraser — soft pencils should be used to avoid damage to the chart and to enable pencil lines to be easily erased.

Essential to accurate navigation is a log that records speed and/or distance. This provides a means of measuring distance run in a given time. If possible, purchase and install a recording log that will supply speed and your distance run in nautical miles.

Use a notebook or ship's log book to record events and times used in plotting a course and fixing position.

It is always advisable each season to motor the boat over the measured mile so you can calibrate and correct your log if necessary.

Knowing how to plot a course and fix your position brings satisfaction in being able to safely negotiate coastlines.

Plotting equipment includes dividers and a set of parallel rules — clear plastic rules are best. Your track has now to be converted to a series of courses to steer. Set one edge of the parallel rules along each track line in succession and step or roll it across to the middle or centre of the compass rose. Read off the magnetic course on the inner magnetic ring in the direction of your track.

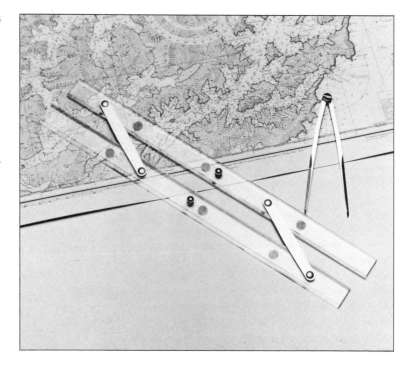

how you plot a course

On any trip — even a short hop — it is a good idea to plot a course on the appropriate chart and keep an hour-by-hour log. In this way you will be able to have a good idea of your position at any given time. Not only is this good practice, but it could be extremely helpful on that day when an unexpected rain squall suddenly descends and obliterates all trace of land for half an hour or so.

First, mark your point of departure (harbour entrance, wharf etc.) on the chart with a circled dot. From this point, use a soft pencil and the parallel rules to draw the track you want to follow. The track will take the form of a series of straight lines from departure point to destination and will avoid rocks and islands, reefs and shoals, land generally and any other immovable objects. Take care to leave the harbour, estuary or river mouth in the prescribed manner (port marker to starboard side of the vessel).

Next you need to calculate the distance of each leg of the course in order to estimate the approximate time each leg should take, depending upon your speed. With this information you will then know when to change course even if you are unable to check your position with a fix. (If possible, course changes should be made near and abeam the island, reef, etc. you are going around in order that a fix can be easily made at that point.)

On all charts, distance is measured from the latitude scale at the sides of the chart. Each degree of latitude is divided into 60 minutes, each minute is equal to one nautical mile. Using a pair of dividers, set the two points one at each end of the track leg and measure off the length against the latitude scale. The longitude scale at the top and bottom of charts is never used to measure distance.

By noting the time of your departure and knowing your speed, you will be able to calculate at what time your first change of course should be made. If, for example, the first leg from the point of departure was 10 nautical miles and your speed was 5 knots, then you would be due to change course after 2 hours.

However, this calculation makes no allowance for the effects of wind, leeway and tidal flow. You could spend a long time at night school working out the effects of all these factors, but for most of the sailing you will do, all you really need to know are the times of high and low water. If you know that the leg of the course you are on is against the tidal flow, then obviously you are going to be slowed somewhat. If the tide is running in the direction of your course, then your speed will be increased. If the tide is striking abeam your course, you are going to be pushed sideways. Every trip you make will be affected by tidal flow and it is a factor that you will come to automatically take into account.

The leeway your boat makes is something you will learn from experience, and will be able to pretty accurately estimate its effect on your track. On average, leeway will add from 5° to 10° on your course.

This then is 'dead reckoning', calculating the boat's position by considering the course steered and the distance run, allowing for leeway, current, etc. It will not give you a precise position — there are too many variables such as how accurately you have steered and the natural factors already mentioned — but it is obvious that its accuracy is improved if you do keep a good hour-by-hour log of course steered and distance run.

Most of the navigation you do can rely on visual sighting and dead reckoning. Your position can be checked by taking a fix but with most coastal cruising, dead reckoning will suffice.

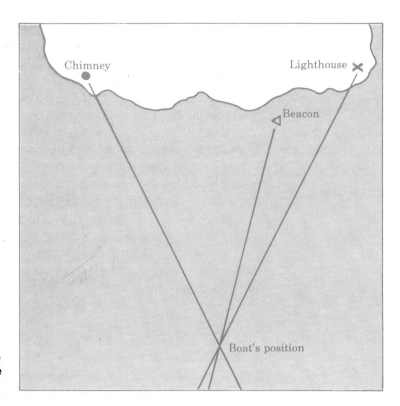

Plotting a bearing from the intersection of two or three lines of bearing.

plotting a bearing

Your position is fixed, or determined, by the intersection of two or more lines of bearing. In the case of coastal cruising, these bearings would be taken on points of land, beacons, navigation lights.

To fix a position from the land, you need to be able to take at least two simultaneous bearings on objects sufficiently wide apart to give a large angle at the point their positional lines intersect. The nearer the angle is to 90°, the more accurate the fix. With two bearings, ideally the angle should approach a right angle; if taking three bearings — which is more accurate — then the angles between each of the lines can be about 60°.

From your chart you should be able to sort out at least two identifiable landmarks or navigation lights (these identified by their colour(s), grouping of lights and frequency and sequence of flashing) to take bearings on. Using a hand-bearing compass, hold it at eye level with the prism on the side opposite your eye. Adjust the prism so you can see the compass card and lubberline reflected in it. The compass bowl must be kept level as you sight the object across the V sight. Allow the compass to steady itself and then read off the bearing under the lubberline reflected in the prism.

Transfer these bearings to the chart by laying one edge of the parallel rules on the magnetic rose on the line of the bearing, and stepping the other edge to the object sighted. Rule a line on the chart along the edge of the rule and repeat the procedure with the second and third bearings. Where the lines intersect is the fixed position of your boat at the time the bearings were taken.

More often than not your new fixed position will differ from your dead reckoning position and you can either re-draw the track from the new position or make an alteration to your course in order to resume the old track. This will be less of a consideration during the daytime when visibility is good and you see where you are going, but at night you will be relying more heavily on your track and fixes to steer a course.

tides

Tides are the result of the difference in the gravitational pull on the rotating earth by the sun and the moon. A horizontal and vertical force is created that causes the seas to move across the surface of the earth in tidal streams. The direction of these tidal streams and their rate of flow are marked on charts.

Tidal range is the difference between its height at high water and low water. Range is least (neap) when the sun and moon are at right angles to each other and greatest (spring tide) when they are in conjunction (two days after a new moon), or in opposition (two days after a full moon).

Tide tables provide information on times and heights of tides and enable the skipper to choose the best times for leaving a mooring, approaching a low-water anchorage and so on.

sailing at night

In doing a night passage, it is very important to plan your sailing time so that you are not making a landfall or entering a hazardous harbour in total darkness. While some destinations will have navigational lights to guide you in, others won't and it's always advisable to make any landfall during daylight. If it turns out that you are making better time than planned, it is an easy thing to just reduce sail and to go a bit slower so you can sail straight in when it is daylight.

Before it becomes dark, it is a good idea to check sail

For those big boat owners who undertake more than just day trips along the coast the Global Positioning System of satellite position finding is a must. Even the less expensive systems are a great navigational aid in finding reefs and rocks, and in confirming your course. GPS units are available operated either by battery or by ship's power.

combinations. If you have to change a sail or reef, this is going to be a lot less trouble if done while it's still light. In heavy weather a safety harness should be worn, especially if going forward.

Check your compass light to ensure it is working — they suffer quite a bit from salt water spray — and make sure that torches are handy in the cockpit (although not too close to the compass).

When plotting a course, note on a piece of paper any hazards and lights that will be passed in the night so that these can be checked against your course and distance run. (See the chapter 'Rules of the road' for information on lights you must show if sailing at night.)

navigation lights

Lights are described on charts by a combination of symbols and abbreviations. A full light description will consist of the star symbol with magenta flash followed by the character of the light (fixed, flashing, etc.) the colour (the absence of a colour abbreviation means the light is white), and its elevation and range. For example: star symbol and flash (Fl.R. IOs 34m 8M) flashes red every ten seconds, is thirty four metres high and you can see it for eight nautical miles. Note that height is shown denoted with a lower case m for metres and the range with a capital M for nautical miles.

All bearings of lights are given from seaward and refer to true north. Lights should be positively identified by timing their periods accurately, as well as counting the number of flashes.

CLASS OF LIGHT		International abbreviations	Illustration Period shown ____
21	Fixed *(steady light)*	F	
22	Occulting *(total duration of light more than dark)*		
22	*Single-occulting*	Oc	
27	*Group-occulting* *e.g.*	Oc(2)	
(Ka)	*Composite group-occulting* *e.g.*	Oc(2 +3)	
23a	Isophase *(light and dark equal)*	Iso	
23	Flashing *(total duration of light less than dark)*		
23	*Single-flashing*	Fl	
(Kb)	*Long-flashing (flash 2s or longer)*	L Fl	
28	*Group-flashing* *e.g.*	Fl(3)	
(Kc)	*Composite group-flashing* *e.g.*	Fl (2+1)	
24	Quick *(50 to 79—usually either 50 or 60—flashes per minute)*		
24	*Continuous quick*	Q	
(Kd)	*Group quick* *e.g.*	Q (3)	
25	*Interrupted quick*	IQ	

PUBLISHED WITH PERMISSION OF THE HYDROGRAPHIC OFFICE RNZN

chapter 13

buoyage, beaconage and signals

IN ORDER FOR skippers to manoeuvre their boats safely through harbours and along waterways, there have long been various buoyage and beaconage systems using different colours and shapes to indicate the direction of safe passage. We now use the international system known as the IALA (International Association of Lighthouse Authorities) Maritime Buoyage System. This combines the best of the old Lateral system, which was used by New Zealand along with much of the Commonwealth, and the European Cardinal system. There are, in fact, two IALA systems, System A — to which New Zealand belongs — which is 'red to port', and System B.

lateral marks

These are used in the new System A to define the limits of channels. Buoys and beacons are placed to the left or right of the channel to indicate the proper course. But whether the mark is to be kept to port or starboard depends upon knowing what direction of travel they have been positioned for: a mark on the port side when sailing in one direction will be on the starboard side the other way.

In New Zealand the conventional direction of buoyage through harbours and along waterways is as for entering the channel, so that port marks are to port, and starboard marks to starboard. The reverse applies when leaving any harbour or waterway.

Outside of a harbour, what is known as the 'general direction' applies. This is clockwise around both islands and northwestwards through Cook Strait.

Lateral marks are:

Port — **red** can-shaped buoys, and pillars and spars.

Starboard — **green** cone-shaped buoys, and pillars and spars.

Where a channel divides, preferred, deeper channels are indicated by modified port and starboard markers, which the accompanying diagrams explain. In simple terms you continue to obey red-to-red, green-to-green entering; and green-to-red leaving.

Lateral lights, when lit, have the same colours — Port red, Starboard green.

Conventional direction of buoyage for New Zealand.

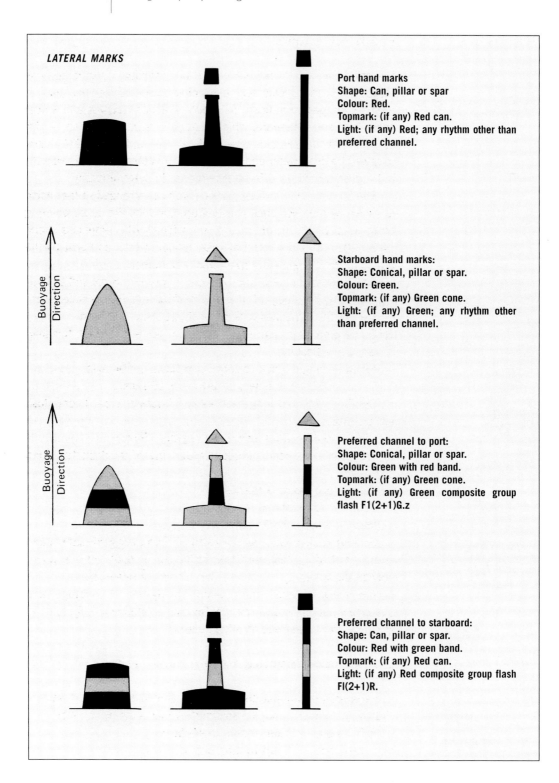

LATERAL MARKS

Port hand marks
Shape: Can, pillar or spar
Colour: Red.
Topmark: (if any) Red can.
Light: (if any) Red; any rhythm other than preferred channel.

Starboard hand marks:
Shape: Conical, pillar or spar.
Colour: Green.
Topmark: (if any) Green cone.
Light: (if any) Green; any rhythm other than preferred channel.

Preferred channel to port:
Shape: Conical, pillar or spar.
Colour: Green with red band.
Topmark: (if any) Green cone.
Light: (if any) Green composite group flash Fl(2+1)G.z

Preferred channel to starboard:
Shape: Can, pillar or spar.
Colour: Red with green band.
Topmark: (if any) Red can.
Light: (if any) Red composite group flash Fl(2+1)R.

Buoyage Direction

Buoyage Direction

cardinal marks

System A cardinal marks are posted on individual dangers such as rocks, reefs and shoals and use colours and the arrangement of topmark shapes to indicate in which direction deepest and safest water lies, and, therefore, which side you should pass them — for example, on the east side of a cardinal mark indicating east. There may well be deep water and safe passage in other quadrants as well, but a chart would need to be referred to, to determine this.

The topmarks of cardinal marks have been arranged so that north is shown by the two cones pointing up; south by the cones pointing down; west by the points of the cones facing (the wineglass shape they make reminding you that they indicate west); and east by the points of the cones facing away from each other.

The colour scheme of the markers themselves is related to their topmarks, as a study of them will show — for example south cardinal-points on cones face down, black band at bottom.

All cardinal mark lights, when lit, are white and quick flashing, or very quick flashing.

North — single quick or very quick flash, continuous.

East — 3VQ every 5 secs or 3Q every 10 secs.

South — 6VQ + 1 long flash every 15 secs or 6Q + 1 long flash every 15 secs.

West — 9VQ every 10 secs or 9Q every 15 secs.

These can be remembered by thinking of a clock face and compass:

East — 3 o'clock, 3 flashes

South — 6 o'clock, 6 flashes

West — 9 o'clock, 9 flashes.

System A also includes marks for isolated dangers, safe water, and special items that are of no navigational significance and can only be explained by your chart (for example a pipeline).

For more detailed information on System A buoyage and beaconage, refer to the Marine Division's publication *Systems of Buoyage and Beaconage for New Zealand.*

ships manoeuvring by horns or siren

In harbours or shipping channels, you should be aware of horn or siren signals, which may be sounded by manoeuvring vessels:

* One hoot — 'I am turning to starboard'
* Two hoots — 'I am turning to port'

These marks take their name from the quadrant in which they are placed and indicate the safe side of a danger on which to pass — e.g. north of a north mark, the deepest water in an area, or draw attention to a bend, junction, bifurcation or the end of a shoal. Shape, colour, topmark and lights for cardinal marks are shown on the diagram. Marks are coloured yellow and black. Yellow is shown in these diagrams by white areas.

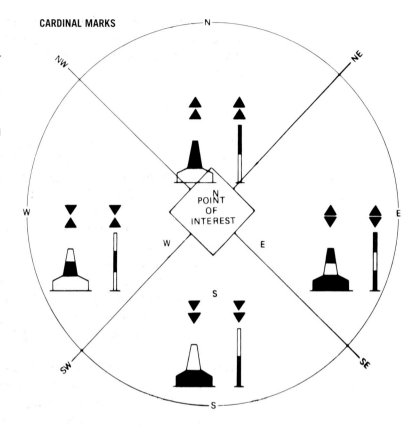

CARDINAL MARKS

* Three hoots — 'I am going astern'
* A series of short blasts — 'Get out of my way'.

(As a memory aid, try 'I wouldn't give TWO HOOTS for a glass of PORT': remember this one and you will probably remember them all.)

Don't panic when a vessel blows its horn as its master is only advising you what he is going to do, and only if you are in the way will you have to change course.

In fog — a rare occurrence for the New Zealand yachtie — vessels may use the following sound signals to indicate their intentions:

* One prolonged blast at intervals of not more than two minutes — 'Making way through the water'
* Two prolonged blasts at intervals of not more than two minutes — 'Stopped and making no way through the water'
* Bell rung rapidly for five seconds at intervals of not more than

one minute — 'At anchor'

* One prolonged blast followed by two short blasts at intervals of not more than two minutes — 'Making way through the water' or 'Under way through water but stopped and making no way through the water'.

signal flags

Because you will frequently be sailing in the same area as manoeuvring ships and fishing boats, it is important to know how to decipher their intentions. In a harbour they are usually moving in confined waters and you must keep well clear.

All ships at anchor will have a black ball hoisted on the bow and even if you can't see the anchor, if the ball is up then the ship's at anchor and not manoeuvring.

All shipping uses an international code of signal flags, each of which has a name and meaning. They are flown when a signal is sent. When hoists of two flags are used the upper one is always read first. When three or more flags are hoisted together on one halyard, the meaning can be found only by looking up the International Code of Signals.

One of the flags you should be most aware of in coastal sailing is that indicating the presence of divers. Should you see this flag flying, keep well clear. If you are already too close, slow down and keep a lookout for surfacing divers. The International Code flag A supersedes the NZ Diver's flag, but either one indicates a diver below or in the vicinity.

Another flag to watch for is the T flag (coloured red, white and blue), which signals that the boat is pair trawling: beware of a net being trawled between it and another boat.

See following pages for depiction of alphabetical signal flags.

Alphabetical flags, with single letter meanings and numeral pennants. Each letter of the alphabet except 'R' is a complete signal when displayed individually. Flag signalling is normally used only for code signals.

A
Blue and white
I have a diver down; keep well clear at slow speed.

B
Red
I am taking in, or discharging, or carrying dangerous goods.

C
Blue stripes top/base, red middle
Yes (affirmative or "the significance of the previous group should be read in the affirmative").

D
Yellow top/base, blue middle
Keep clear of me; I am manoeuvring with difficulty.

E
Blue top, red base
I am altering my course to starboard.

F
Red diamond on white
I am disabled; communicate with me.

G
Yellow and blue stripes, from left
I require a pilot.
When made by fishing vessels operating in close proximity on the fishing grounds it means "I am hauling nets".

H
White, red, from left
I have a pilot on board.

I
Black circle on yellow
I am altering my course to port.

J
Blue top/base, white middle
I am on fire and have dangerous cargo on board: keep well clear of me.

K
Yellow, blue, from left
I wish to communicate with you.

L
Black and yellow squares
You should stop your vessel instantly.

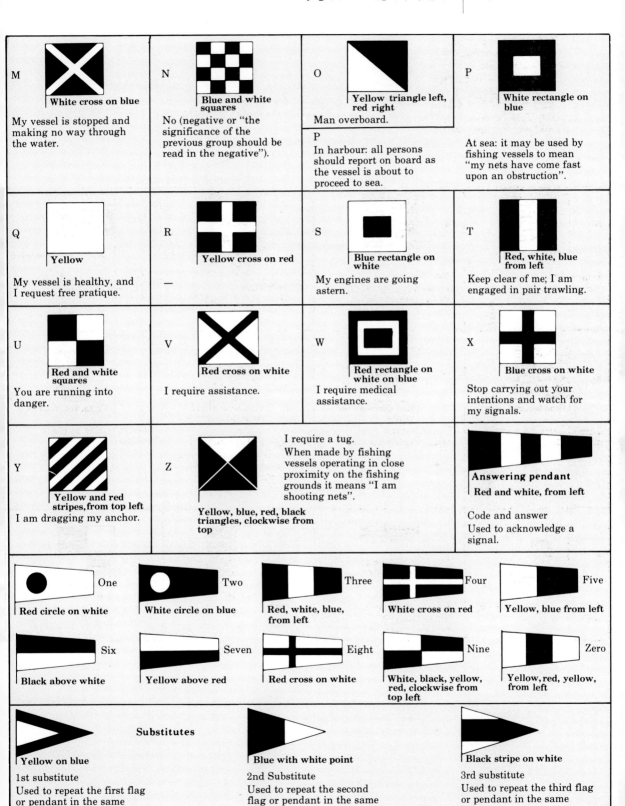

M White cross on blue — My vessel is stopped and making no way through the water.	**N** Blue and white squares — No (negative or "the significance of the previous group should be read in the negative").	**O** Yellow triangle left, red right — Man overboard. **P** In harbour: all persons should report on board as the vessel is about to proceed to sea.	**P** White rectangle on blue — At sea: it may be used by fishing vessels to mean "my nets have come fast upon an obstruction".
Q Yellow — My vessel is healthy, and I request free pratique.	**R** Yellow cross on red — —	**S** Blue rectangle on white — My engines are going astern.	**T** Red, white, blue from left — Keep clear of me; I am engaged in pair trawling.
U Red and white squares — You are running into danger.	**V** Red cross on white — I require assistance.	**W** Red rectangle on white on blue — I require medical assistance.	**X** Blue cross on white — Stop carrying out your intentions and watch for my signals.
Y Yellow and red stripes, from top left — I am dragging my anchor.	**Z** Yellow, blue, red, black triangles, clockwise from top	I require a tug. When made by fishing vessels operating in close proximity on the fishing grounds it means "I am shooting nets".	**Answering pendant** Red and white, from left — Code and answer Used to acknowledge a signal.

One Red circle on white	**Two** White circle on blue	**Three** Red, white, blue, from left	**Four** White cross on red	**Five** Yellow, blue from left
Six Black above white	**Seven** Yellow above red	**Eight** Red cross on white	**Nine** White, black, yellow, red, clockwise from top left	**Zero** Yellow, red, yellow, from left

Substitutes

Yellow on blue — 1st substitute Used to repeat the first flag or pendant in the same hoist.	Blue with white point — 2nd Substitute Used to repeat the second flag or pendant in the same hoist.	Black stripe on white — 3rd substitute Used to repeat the third flag or pendant in the same hoist.

chapter 14

mooring and anchoring

MOORING AND ANCHORING manoeuvres should be carried out under power and at a slow speed to allow time for accurate positioning. As well, the skipper must give consideration to the effects of wind and tide, and the presence of boats and other hazards, and ensure that he or she will be able eventually to leave the mooring or anchorage easily. Speed will give you greater control in these manoeuvres but you should be sure you have adequate reverse power available if needed.

mooring

Whether you are mooring at a traditional buoyed mooring, between a pair of piles, alongside a wharf or sea wall, or at a marina pontoon, the basics of mooring are the same. These include a careful assessment of your approach and the effect that wind, tides, natural drift, and the turning characteristics of your craft may have on your course; and that you have adequate mooring lines. Crew should be prepared for picking up mooring lines or jumping onto the dockside with them.

If you are in unfamiliar waters, check your chart for hazards and ascertain the state of the tide: it may be necessary to check mooring lines frequently after you have first tied up to piles or a wharf to ensure they are sufficient for a rising tide.

A mooring buoy should be approached at reduced speed and heading dead to windward or heading against the tide, whichever is the strongest force. This will further help to slow your speed and allow the skipper to position the boat for the crew to lean over and pick up the buoy. When the helmsman can see that the crew has connected with the buoy, he or she can then reverse or put the boat ahead to help the crew in getting the chain aboard.

Have an escape route planned so that if the first pass is unsuccessful you can continue away from the mooring and come around for a second try. You shouldn't be committed absolutely to having to pick the mooring up first time.

If you over-run a mooring buoy, put the engine into neutral to prevent it fouling the propeller. Wait for the buoy to pop up before going round on it again.

It's a good idea for the novice to practise picking up and leaving on an unoccupied buoy rather than attempt it first time among other boats.

Your requirements for tying up between mooring piles or at a wharf jetty or sea wall include bow and stern lines, forward and aft spring lines, and at least two fenders at the best position and height to protect the topsides of the boat. The spring lines will stop any backward or forward motion. Fenders will take the shock as the boat is manoeuvred against the wharf or jetty and protect the topsides once it is moored. Fenders should be attached to secure points at the deck sides such as cleats and the bases of stanchions, but not to lifelines if it can be avoided.

Where ropes rub against the edges of mooring piles or the dockside, they should be protected from chafing. If mooring outside another boat, take your own lines to the wharf or jetty.

If rafting up against another boat, spring lines are taken from one boat's capshroud to the other's cockpit, and vice versa. As well, breast lines are fixed between cockpits and capshrouds. Place fenders between the topside to prevent rubbing. To avoid rigging and spars fouling each other, raft together with hulls slightly offset.

Coming into a marina the main consideration is to stop the boat going any further forward into its berth. Motor slowly parallel to the jetty arm and turn into your berth from a position that allows a wide swing in. The main consideration is to stop the boat going any further forward than necessary, so the crew will pick up and attach stern lines first then bow lines. A short burst astern on the engine will assist in slowing passage into the berth. Spring lines are not necessary in a marina, but a breast line would be tied to the berth jetty for ease of getting aboard.

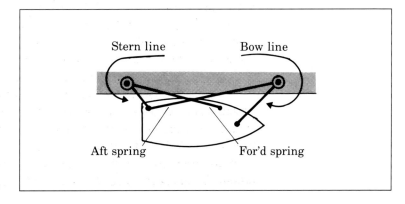

Mooring between poles or at a wharf jetty or sea wall.

CQR plough anchor.

Danforth anchor.

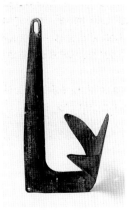

Bruce anchor.

The main consideration in tying up is to first attach windward lines. Other lines can follow.

When reversing out of a marina berth, push the tiller away from the direction you want to go; a wheel is turned towards the desired direction. Initially, it may help if you stand forward of the wheel, face aft and steer as you would normally but with the stern replacing the bow.

anchoring

This is one job on a boat that does require a bit of muscle and often speed, and on a lot of boats it is much the best thing if a male looks after the laying and raising of the anchor and a female takes the helm.

Your boat should carry a heavy anchor attached to a length of heavy chain at least as long as your boat. The chain is even more important than the anchor in achieving a successful anchorage and lay.

Your local chandler will advise on the best weight of anchor and chain, and thickness of warp for your boat.

The CQR plough anchor or Danforth anchor is recommended for most sailing around New Zealand's coasts for its ability in digging down into most seabed types; its hinged, angled shank helps it to bite in.

The anchor is best stowed below deck to avoid fouling sheets and dirtying sails, as well as preventing stubbed toes of crew working at the bow.

Bow fittings should be robust enough to carry the chain and rope from any angle without them riding up out of the bow fairlead or pulling it away from its attachment points: the pressure exerted on the bow by the anchor warp in a confused, heavy sea can be great.

As with mooring, if you are in unfamiliar waters check your chart for information on possible hazards such as power cables and for suitable anchorages. If anchoring near other boats, check their swinging pattern and keep a good distance away. Leave room for manoeuvring when it comes time to pick up the anchor and leave.

If paying the anchor out by hand, lay out the chain on the foredeck and make sure the rope is ready to run free. Head into the wind to slow the boat and when stopped or in slow reverse, lower the anchor gently over the bow hand-over-hand, letting the chain and warp through the fairlead, and allow the boat to drift back. When you hear all of the chain go over the bow, put the boat into slow reverse to bite the anchor flukes in to the bottom. Drift downwind sufficiently to lay the chain flat on the bottom. Ensure that the anchor isn't dragging by checking the boat's position against landmarks or other anchored craft.

A good guide to the amount of warp required is to allow five times the depth of water under the boat.

If the anchor is dragging, let out a little more warp and if it persists, consider it's probably worth re-anchoring: the dragging may be due to a fouled anchor.

To pick up the anchor when leaving, motor forward slowly in the direction of the warp, taking care not to run over it. Break out the anchor from the bottom, and pull chain and warp aboard. If the anchor has fouled, try one of two things to release it. The first is to motor around the warp in a circle at a suitable distance from the anchor spot — you may have to let out a little rope if you have already motored right up over the anchor — keeping tension on the warp and now and then going astern to try to dislodge it. If that doesn't work try taking in as much warp as possible, applying tension and then suddenly letting it go, the shock of which may suddenly release the anchor; or try slowly motoring over the top of the anchor.

The amount of boat speed necessary when raising anchor will depend on wind strength.

A second anchor will rarely be needed — in nearly three years of global cruising I had occasion to lay a second anchor just once — but conditions of high wind or rolling swells may necessitate it. The second anchor can be a grapnel or plough type and this should be stowed under a forward bunk and secured to the stringers there. In the case of high winds and a yacht unable to change its anchorage to a safer site, the second anchor is rowed out and set at an angle to the main anchor. If anchored in a bay when there is a strong rolling swell coming in, the second anchor set out from the stern so that the boat is held face facing the swell.

If you are alone aboard a yacht and it starts to drag ashore, just put the motor into slow ahead and motor out of danger with the anchor and warp still down.

Strong winds and an insecure mooring can result in damage to your boat, even loss.

trip preparation and cabin life

THE AMOUNT OF GEAR you can take along on a sailing trip, be it a one-day outing or something longer, is governed by the limitations of space aboard.

clothing

For a day's outing, if the weather threatens to be wet or cold (if there is wind it will always be cold), you'll need a wet-weather jacket and possibly a change of clothing, but keep in mind the stowage factor of the boat you're on. You'll always be surprised at what do can do without.

One towel per person is usually enough. A length of cotton material is excellent for drying off with after a swim — it dries quickly, doesn't hold the sand like a towel and packs easily. If the weather is good, you'll find that you'll live in your swimming attire and a T-shirt. Sunglasses and Factor 15 UV cream are very important. So is a visor or hat.

In wet weather, shorts and wet-weather jacket are much preferable to long trousers. If you are wearing trousers and it turns wet, swap the trousers for shorts and save the former for when the weather is merely cold.

The quality of today's warm clothing for sailing has greatly reduced the huge pile of jerseys and parkas that used to clutter up the underdecks of many a yacht. Deck shoes should always be worn aboard any yacht.

stowage

Stowage is at a premium on most yachts and whether you're going out for the day or for a month, all your gear is most easily carried in soft sea-bags. Because these keep everything totally zipped in, there's nothing loose or protruding to fall out as gear is passed aboard the boat and down the companionway.

If your trip is for a weekend or longer, one sea-bag can contain the stores, clothes can be put in another, bedding in another and so on. This way everything is kept tidy and together.

Sailing gloves provide protection in cold conditions while leaving the fingers free for fiddly jobs.

Diagram of stowage.

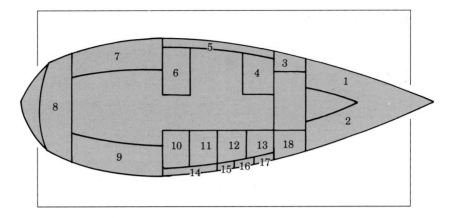

When changing your clothing, make sure you put unwanted items back in your bag. Anything left lying around in the cabin or cockpit is liable to be packed away in a locker by the skipper, and you'll forget it and go home without it. Individual gear should be placed where it can be reached without disturbing others.

A good idea when storing food and clothing aboard is to draw a sketch of all the locker storage on your boat. Give each locker a number and then note down exactly what has been put in each. This provides a quick-find system when someone wants something in a hurry. Of course, it must be kept up to date.

children

Always carry lifejackets for any children sailing with you. If the children are very young and not used to boating, they should be kept in lifejackets all the time to release the skipper from the responsibility of their safety. Even when rowing them about in a dinghy (unless you are assured of the children's boating confidence and their own responsibility), you should make them wear lifejackets.

When it comes to feeding babies and young children aboard, it must be remembered that their stomachs are a lot more sensitive than those of adult crew. Babies are particularly vulnerable and you must ensure the highest standards of cleanliness. It is a good idea to carry bottled water for them, or boil, cool and bottle as you go. This is a sensible precaution for young children as well.

Canned baby foods, disposable feeding bottles and disposable nappies have all made the yachting parent's life a lot easier these days, as have the wide range of juices available.

food

When going out for a day's sailing, it is usual for everyone to bring along something to pool for lunch. Take enough for your own requirements and a bit for someone else.

For longer trips, it is advisable to pre-cook a certain amount of food and store it in vacuum-packed plastic bags. (Dishes, foil tins and rigid plastic containers are to be avoided, again because of limited stowage.)

Grocery shopping for the boat will be the same as for home, except that convenience will be more important than cost. Meals should be able to be quickly put together and not require lots of cooking and extras. If you have a good freezer aboard, vacuum pack everything for saving space and ease of thawing.

Freeze-dried foods are good as a back-up. Take curries, peas, beans, rice risottos and macaronis. A can of tomatoes, pineapple or corned beef added to most of these makes a more interesting and tasty meal.

Bread will not keep fresh for long (raisin loaf lasts better than ordinary bread if wrapped in brown paper), so take crackers instead. These can be a complete bread substitute, and are good for breakfast and lunch. For weekend trips, bread can be taken along and stored in the freezer.

Vegetables are most important but unfortunately are difficult to keep. Some like lots of air, some like none, some like a cool place. Cabbage is a great standby and wrapped in brown paper will keep in a good condition for a considerable time. Without a refrigerator, lettuce is a mess after about the second day. I keep vegetables in a large camper's safe.

Take milk powder rather than liquid milk, and make it up as you need it. Long-life milk, like the bottled variety, is likely to spill everywhere once it is opened, unless used all at once.

first aid

If you are unsure whether of not you'll be a good sailor, take sea-sickness prevention before leaving; Marzine is good. Never feel ashamed about taking this precaution. Wrist bands with pressure points are good if you prefer not to take a tablet. Carry sunblock and burn creams and something to prevent windburn to the lips (they can really suffer). A visor or hat is also necessary, as are good sunglasses to prevent glare and eyestrain.

entertainment

You will not always be able — or even want — to be up on deck or adventuring ashore, so it's a good idea to take along a variety of lazy and rainy-day entertainments. A pack of cards provides lots of relaxing fun. Make sure you also have a fair range of games so everyone can join in. If each person takes a couple of paperbacks, you'll be able to swap them around, and if there's room aboard, you could also bring your hobby with you. I take line for making macrame hangings, paints and a sketch book, embroidery, even a recipe book. Other people take whittling tools, wood and lino carving equipment, and musical instruments (if you play any kind of instrument reasonably well you can be assured your music will be welcome).

Early nights seem to be the thing when you're away cruising. All that sea air leaves you pleasantly tired, and it's hard on the ship's batteries if you use the boat's lights for late night reading. Get up early and go to bed early.

toilet

If the boat you are sailing on is fitted with a marine toilet, it's a good idea to get the skipper to brief you on its operation. A lot of these types of toilet are difficult to use and if they are not operated correctly, they tend to allow water back into the boat. In the confined quarters aboard a boat there's not much privacy so if you're in any doubt, ask how the toilet works first — better than getting the skipper in afterwards.

A sea-cock (or gate valve and skin fitting) is the device that operates the toilet inlet and outlet. To close it, you wind away clockwise until all daylight has been shut out; this stops it siphoning up water from outside the hull.

Some toilets do not have a turn off gate valve. Check with your skipper.

It's sensible to be cautious about using a marine toilet: more boats sink annually due to marine toilet failure than any other cause. When you use one, make sure it has finished siphoning and the shut-off lever is properly closed so as not to let any more water into the toilet.

Toilet odours can readily be got rid of by lighting a match and then extinguishing it: the fumes from the burning match-head will effectively disguise any other smells. Keep a box of matches in the toilet for this purpose.

galley

Cooking burners in the galley may burn gas, kerosene or methylated spirits. While gas is a highly explosive fuel, it tends to be the one yachties prefer. It is fast to cook with, clean-burning, efficient, economical and easy to obtain. And you can smell it if you get a leak. But remember it is explosive, and you must respect this and take precautions when using it.

The gas bottle should be stored in a separate enclosure and there should be a drain out of this enclosure venting outside the boat so that if any gas leaks, it won't go into the bilges, which is your main worry.

There should be a tap on the line between the bottle and the stove. Every two months, make a thick soap and water solution and 'paint' it around the gas-line connections. If it bubbles you have a gas leak at the joints. Check and repair.

Get into the habit of turning the gas on and off at the bottle as well as at the stove. Every time you use the stove, turn it on at the bottle, then on at the stove. Off at the stove, then off at the bottle. Stick up a little sign above the stove that says 'Turn the gas off at the bottle' to remind yourself and particularly any other people using it.

With all stoves, no matter what the fuel, keep a fire extinguisher nearby.

water

Water tanks are filled using a non-toxic hose. If the water on board tastes bad, it is probably because the wrong hose was used. An ordinary hose will become lined with bugs and a filmy slime, which taints the water. This doesn't occur with a non-toxic hose, which has a special liner.

Like the boat's batteries, the water supply needs to be conserved if you are cruising for a period. Use only what you need. Clean your teeth using water in a cup, not with running water. Wash dishes and clothes in salt water then rinse in fresh. Every time you go ashore, take a plastic jerrycan and fill it with water to replenish the tanks on board.

A solar shower is well worthwhile. You fill it up, lay it out on the deck in the sun for an hour or so, and you then have enough hot water to provide a shower for several adults. You can hang it up over the cockpit and have a real shower, with the space to move your arms around and so on. A built-in shower below decks is pretty much a waste of money and valuable space. A portable solar shower does the job better and costs less. It is also great value for camping. When cruising, you can take the shower with you when you go ashore, and fill it up from a stream or other water supply, instead of getting into the boat's fresh water supply. Nylon carpet through the cabin is not only hard-wearing but also dries fast. If it's wet, just give it a shake outside, lay it down again, and it's as good as dry.

galley hints

* Have a fire extinguisher near to the stove in case of cooking fires. A packet of bicarbonate of soda is also useful in putting out grease or fat fires.

* Use up leftovers quickly. Reheating meat can lead to food poisoning, especially during the summer. Beware of canned or bottled foods that smell 'off' — they probably are. Don't eat them. Also take care eating any foods that have been thawed out for too long.

* Pour molten cooking fats into an empty tin can — never a plastic or cardboard cup. When it has set solid, the fat and the can are thrown into the rubbish.

* Keep all food out of the sun.

* Always take great care in cleaning out food containers so that they are spotless and germ-free, and be similarly severe in throwing out any foods that have gone bad.

* The refrigerator can be kept smelling fresh by occasionally wiping it out with a little vanilla essence on a damp cloth.

* Sherry can be used to enliven soups and stews. Lemon juice is useful to give flavour to not-so-fresh vegetables and to prevent sliced fruits such as apple and banana from going brown.

* Plastic bags are enormously useful, not only for storage but also in the preparation of meals. Salads, for example, can be tossed without making a mess by putting the salad ingredients and the dressing into a large plastic bag and then shaking it. Again, to coat meat pieces with flour, the meat, flour and any dried herbs can all be placed inside a plastic bag and then the bag swung around. Tie the mouths of plastic bags closed with 'twisties' or clothes-pegs.

* Vegetables should be stored in well-ventilated storage bins. Deep wire trays are ideal. A laundry basket is another good way of storing vegetables for long life. Check regularly on the condition of your vegetables and throw out any that are soft. Cut off the leaves and shoots of root vegetables to prevent them growing and drawing

A cone-shaped stainless steel kettle boils quickly because of its large base area and narrow top. It won't readily spill and there is no top to lose — advantages in a ship's galley.

the goodness away from the vegetable! (I have a camp safe and hang it up forward.)

* Fresh salad vegetables like cucumbers and lettuce will keep longer if they are not washed, packed into brown bags and then kept in a cool place.

* The fewer galley utensils you can get away with, the better. Cook as many meals as possible in the one pot or pan. A wok is useful here and a pressure cooker is another quick, economical means of cooking meats and vegetables together.

* An insulated polystyrene picnic box is a boon for warm-weather sailing. It makes an admirable ice-box for small yachts without proper refrigerators and provides increased cool storage for yachts already with a fridge.

* Wide-mouthed vacuum flasks are excellent for storing cooked foods in. These can be made ahead of time when you are already at the stove and then kept in the flasks until lunch or even dinner. Or stored for taking ashore on picnics. Use them for soups, stews and anything that will pour.

* If the soup or stew you have made is too salty, it can be saved by adding one or two raw potatoes which have been cut in half. The potatoes will absorb the excess salt: They are discarded before serving the meal.

* Dispose of rubbish by compressing all packets, tins etc, as small as possible and take home with you. Never throw anything over the side that fish cannot eat.

* An enamel cup in the galley is always handy as foods can be both mixed in it and heated up, and that is especially useful if you have young children aboard.

lighting

Conserve the boat's batteries by using kerosene lanterns or candles whenever possible, and make a point of turning off unused electric lights. If you want to read in your bunk at night, the skipper will appreciate your supplying your own torch and batteries.

crewing

If you have been asked to crew on a boat, there are certain things which most skippers will expect and appreciate of you on board their boat.

Probably the most important thing is make sure you can be told what to do, to follow what is asked of you, and not give advice to the skipper. Most likely you will be given control of the mainsheet or of letting go the leeward jib sheet. The helmsman will always give the command to 'go about' and it's then up to you to ensure you let the leeward sheet go at the right moment, or to adjust the mainsheet as necessary.

When you are sure the leeward sheet is free, you can often help in tailing on the other side, or perhaps trimming the mainsheet.

Remember that after each tack the leeward sheet should be coiled from the cleated end in big even loops and laid out flat in the cockpit. You'll be an even more valuable crew member if you keep the cockpit tidy and free of unnecessary gear that could get in the way.

In addition:

* Shoes — Crew should wear clean white-soled shoes on deck, never black-soled ones. Bring the shoes to the boat and put them on there, rather than wear dirty shoes aboard. Decks and sails mark very easily and it's often impossible to get marks out of them. Shoes will protect the sailor from stubbing toes on stanchions, slide tracks and other deck fittings. And if decks are wet, bare feet can be a liability.

* Smoking — As far as I am concerned, smoking is a prohibited act aboard boats, for reasons of the comfort of the rest of the crew and to protect sails. Cigarette ash can leave discolorations on sails, and sparks from a pipe can be carried by the wind to burn pinholes in them. Below decks, the cabin is too confined an area to be able to afford a smoker. Apart from the immediate inconvenience of a fuggy atmosphere, the smell of cigarette smoke quickly finds its way into pillows and blankets and clothes where it has a long life.

* Swimming — Always make sure your towel is in the cockpit before you go for a swim off the boat so that you won't drip water through the cabin searching for it.

* Topsides — Always respect a boat's topsides — that area between the waterline and the deck. When picking up the anchor, pull up the last bit gently to avoid the anchor swinging and hitting the bow. If anything has to be thrown overboard, it must be thrown to leeward and well away from the topsides.

If you are a skipper and frequently sailing with novice crews, or have a young family that is gradually being introduced to sailing, it is a good idea to attach named sticky identity labels to blocks, pulleys and cleats to help the crew quickly find their way around.

sailing shorthanded

If sailing with just a couple of adults aboard, you must work out methods of hoisting and dropping sails that are manageable, efficient and safe. The person on the helm is the key to success here, and she or he must be confident in being able to steer a course and hold it. Once this is done the matter of adding or taking off sail is a simple one.

When hoisting the mainsail, the helmsman should head to wind as usual then set the mainsheet to the desired course before the person at the mast hoists. Once the sail has been winched up tight, the helmsman then goes onto course.

In hoisting the headsail, the helmsman takes the boat up a bit, which makes hoisting easier for the person forward. The person in the cockpit sets the jib sheet and goes back onto course.

As usual, when hoisting halyards, pull them up hand-over-hand then tension on the winch. Self-tailing winches or ones with the cleat cast into the winch are ideal for shorthanded sailing. Otherwise, put the usual turns on the winch and winch with one hand while putting weight on the halyard tail with the other.

Getting the headsail off, especially in strong winds, is done with the helmsman holding the jib sheet in one hand while the person at the mast uncleats the jib halyard and releases it on a cue from the helmsman as he or she quickly heads to wind and spins off the jib sheet. The helmsman then goes back on course again. Another excellent method which we use in any sea or wind is to bear dead flat off the wind and quickly release the halyard at a cue from the helmsman when he or she sees the headsail come back to the centreline of the boat.

Using these methods, there is no need for the person at the mast to go forward of the mast and wrestle with a dangerously flapping headsail. It can be fully dropped from the mast and then the masthand can go forward to disconnect the halyard from the head of the sail.

Once the headsail has been attended to, the boat can be brought head to wind by the helmsman and the person at the mast then lets go of the main halyard to drop the mainsail. He or she strops down the halyard — using a boathook if necessary — then both the helmsman and masthand furl the sail together.

chapter 16

the boat code

SECTION 1
Part 1 rules of the road

AS WITH DRIVING, there are rules of the road which must be obeyed, and failure to comply with these means that you can be prosecuted and fined. These are contained in the Collision Regulations. Whether you own a dinghy, yacht or motor boat, you are legally obligated to know the rules and obey them.

rules
In all, there are 38 rules and four annexes to the Collision Regulations. Below are some of the major rules.

lookout *(rule 5)*
Every vessel shall at all times maintain by all available means a proper lookout to avoid collision.

Although this seems obvious, this rule is so often broken. Some vessels have blind spots such as a power boat on the plane with its bow up, or a low cut headsail on a yacht. More recently, problems have occurred with pleasure craft being controlled by automatic pilot, with the crew distracted doing other things.

safe speed *(rule 6)*
Every vessel shall at all times proceed at a safe speed so as to take effective action to avoid collision. In determining a safe speed, the following factors should be taken into account: visibility, other vessels in the vicinity, your manoeuvrability, distracting lights at night, the wind and sea conditions, the available depth of water.

risk of collision *(rule 7)*
Every vessel shall use all appropriate means to avoid a collision. There are two methods of determining whether you are on a collision course:

1. Compass bearing: You take a bearing of the other vessel from your boat with a hand-bearing compass. Another bearing is taken a few moment later. If the bearing remains the same, then you are on a collision course. If the bearing increases, the vessel will pass ahead of you and if it decreases then it should pass astern.

2. A simpler method is to line up the approaching vessel with some land behind it, for example, a headland, prominent rock or tree. If the bow of the other vessel appears stationary to the land behind it, you are on a collision course. If the bow appears to move forward of the land, the other vessel will pass ahead of you; if the bow appears to be moving backwards, the vessel will pass astern of you. But remember, if the bow appears to be moving only slowly ahead or astern of the land your courses are very close and you should prepare to take evasive action.

    If there is no land present, line up the approaching vessel with a fixed object — a winch or stanchion — on your own vessel. If the vessel's relative bearing remains constant, you are on a collision course.

With both methods, keep taking bearings or sightings until all likelihood of collision has passed.

action to avoid collision (*rule 8*)
Action to avoid collision must be made in ample time. Don't waste time altering course by only a few degrees. Make your intention very clear well ahead of time. Your change of course should be large enough to be obvious to the other vessel. Alternatively, reduce speed quickly so your intentions are seen by the other vessel. Although this rule applies to every vessel, smaller craft like dinghies should give way to larger boats in crowded areas. Larger boats tend to be more difficult to manoeuvre than smaller craft.

narrow channels (*rule 9*)
(a) A vessel proceeding along a confined channel in a boat harbour, river or fairway shall at all times keep to the starboard side, and pass other vessels port side to port side.
(b) All small craft, power or sail, must also keep out of the way of shipping in a narrow channel.
(c) A vessel engaged in fishing shall not impede the passage of any other vessel navigating within a narrow channel.
(d) Any vessel shall not anchor, except in an emergency, in a narrow channel.

Narrow channels — always keep to the starboard in fairways and confined channels.

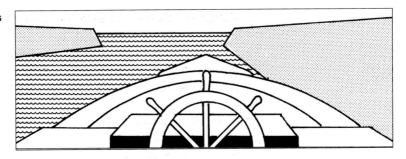

sailing vessels (*rule 12*)

When two sailing boats are approaching on opposite tacks the boat on the port tack (the wind coming over its port or left side) shall give way to the boat on starboard tack.

If both have the wind on the same side, the windward boat will give way. (The windward boat is the one closest to where the wind is coming from.) This rule applies to yachts being propelled only by wind. If the sails are up and the motor is going, the yacht is defined as power driven.

An aid to remembering the sailing collision rule is: Wind coming over the right side (starboard), you are in the right. Wind coming over the left side is your port side. Port is red, red is danger. Change course or give way.

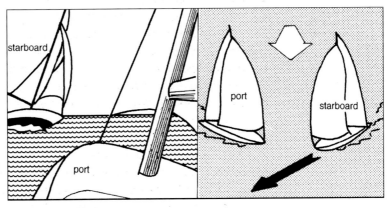

Yachts approaching on opposite tacks — the boat on the starboard tack has right of way.

overtaking (*rule 13*)

Any vessel overtaking another shall keep out of the way of the vessel being overtaken. A vessel is deemed to be overtaking another if it is just aft of the beam of the other.

The vessel being overtaken should maintain its course and speed but if it does alter its course, then the overtaking vessel must still give way.

head-on situation (*rule 14*)

When two power-driven vessels are approaching head-on so as to involve the risk of collision, each vessel will alter course to starboard so that they pass on the port side of each other.

Overtaking — the overtaking vessel must keep out of the way of the vessel being overtaken.

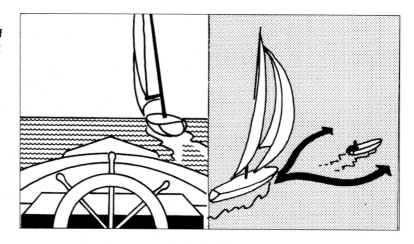

crossing situation (*rule 15*)

When two motor boats are crossing each other's path on a collision course, the vessel that has the other on its starboard or right must give way. (This also applies to yachts under power.)

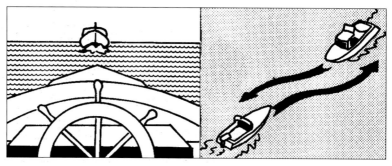

Head-on situation — vessels must pass to port.

Crossing — the vessel that has the other on its starboard must give way.

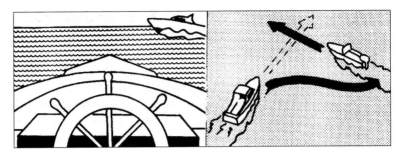

action by vessel holding course (*rule 17*)

Where a vessel has the right of way, it should hold its course and speed unless the other vessel fails to take evasive action.

A common fault with inexperienced skippers is that although they have the right of way, they get nervous and instead of holding course they make erratic alterations that are not only hard to follow but will cause concern aboard the other vessel that under the rules has to give way. Be confident when you have right of way — make your direction intent clear and proceed with caution.

responsibilities between vessels (*rule 18*)

A power-driven vessel will give way to:

- a sailing vessel;
- a vessel engaged in fishing;
- a vessel restricted in its ability to manoeuvre.

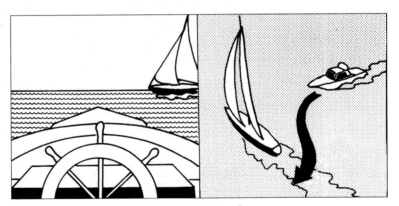

Power-driven vessels must give way to sailing vessels.

A sailing boat will give way to:

- a vessel engaged in fishing;
- another vessel being overtaken;
- a vessel restricted in its ability to manoeuvre.

harbour regulations

All small craft operating in harbours will keep clear of all vessels exceeding 500 tons — for example, a ferry boat on a scheduled service.

No person shall propel or navigate a small craft at a speed exceeding 5 knots:
• within 30 metres of any other vessel, raft or person in the water;
• within 200 metres of the shore or any other structure;
• within 200 metres of any vessel or raft that is flying Flag A of the international signals, which indicates a diver is working.

Note that all of the above apply to jet skis as well as to boats.

Remember your obligations under Rule 6 — Safe Speed, and Rule 13 — Overtaking. If you are overtaking or passing a moored or anchored boat, or crossing the path of another vessel, your speed must not exceed 5 knots. Generally, the safest way of passing a vessel, whether anchored or moving, is to pass astern of it. Remember your speed. Too often today powerful power boats roar close by smaller craft, causing a wash from their wake that sometimes can be dangerous.

Part 2 lights

Under the Collision Regulations all boats must display lights from sunset to sunrise or when visibility is restricted by fog, rain and so on. It is the responsibility of every boat skipper from a small dinghy to a large ocean-going yacht to know how these regulations apply to the boat they operate.

masthead lights

A white light on the centre line of a vessel that can be seen over an arc of 22.50 and fixed so that it may be seen from right ahead to 22.50 aft of the beam on either side of the vessel.

Visibility
Vessel 12 metres but less than 20 metres: 3 miles
Vessel less than 12 metres: 2 miles

sidelights

A green light on the starboard side and a red one on the port side. Each light must be able to be seen over an arc of 112.50 from ahead to 22.50 aft of the beam on its respective side. The sidelights may be combined on the centre line of the vessel, and usually the lantern fitting is positioned on the bow.

Visibility
Vessel over 12 metres: 3 miles
Vessel less than 12 metres: 2 miles

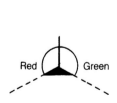

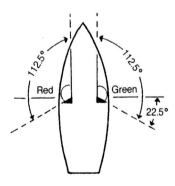

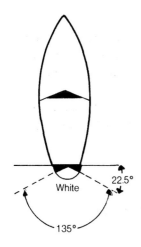

sternlights

A white light position on the stern showing an unbroken light over an arc of 135°.

Visibility
Vessel over 12 metres: 3 miles
Vessel less than 12 metres: 2 miles

all-round white light

A light showing an unbroken light over 360°.

A power-driven vessel less than 7 metres and with a maximum speed of less than 7 knots must display an all-round light or, at the very minimum, have a torch ready to show when approached by another vessel. It may also show sidelights if practical.

A vessel under power less than 12 metres in length but with a maximum speed of over 7 knots must display sidelights, a stern light, and a mast light at least 1 metre in height above the sidelights. Alternatively, it may display sidelights and an all-round white light carried as a fixture on a mast as least 1 metre in height above the sidelights.

Generally, all power-driven vessels over 7 metres and less than 50 must display a masthead forward light, sidelights, and a stern light.

A sailing vessel or a boat under oars less than 7 metres must carry on board an electric torch or lantern showing a white light, which should be shone in sufficient time to prevent a collision. However, they should, where possible, exhibit sidelights and stern lights.

sailing vessels

A sailing vessel under way must display sidelights and a stern light. In a sailing vessel of less than 20 metres, the lights may be carried in one lantern at or near the top of the mast where it can best be seen. It is usually referred to as the tricolour and must have a visibility of 2 miles.

Note: A sailing vessel using its motors with or without sails is deemed a power-driven vessel and cannot display the tricolour.

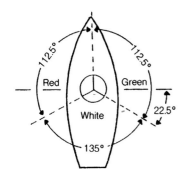

anchored vessels

Any vessel less than 7 metres does not have to exhibit any lights, except in a narrow channel, fairway or where other vessels navigate. Vessels over 7 metres and less than 5 must display an all-round white light.

Any vessel engaged in diving at night must, in addition to the lights already mentioned, display three all-round lights exhibited vertically — red (top), white (middle), and red (bottom).

light signals

manoeuvring and warning signals *(rule 34)*

One flash: I am altering my course to starboard.
Two flashes: I am altering my course to port.
Three flashes: I am going astern.
A flash can be shown by a torch or an all-round light.

Note: Full regulations governing lights to be exhibited by all vessels can be found in the Shipping (distress Signals and Prevention of Collision) Regulation 1988 *published by the Ministry of Transport.*

Part 3 buoys, beacons and signals

New Zealand belongs to an international organisation that has a standardised system for buoys, beacons and signals. The system is called 'System A', which is built around the principle 'red to port, green to starboard' when entering a harbour. In order for skippers to manoeuvre their craft safely through harbours, channels and waterways, they must have a working knowledge of this system. The types of marks are:

- Lateral marks
- Cardinal marks
- Isolated danger marks
- Safe water marks
- Special marks

Each mark is characterised during the day by its colour, shape and topmark, and during the night by the colour and pulse or rhythm of the light it gives out.

lateral marks

These are used to define the limits of channels when entering a port. Buoys and beacons are placed to the left and right of the channel to indicate the proper course to be taken. In New Zealand the direction of the buoyage and beacons for harbour channels and waterways is for entering. This means port buoys and beacons will always be on the left and starboard buoys on the right. Port buoys are always red in colour and starboard buoys are always green. Similarly, lights on lateral buoys and beacons, when lit, have the same colours: port — red, starboard — green.

cardinal marks

Cardinal marks are placed around dangers such as rocks, reefs and shoals, and indicate the northerly, southerly, easterly and westerly limits of the danger and where the navigable water lies. There are four marks, referring to the four quadrants of the compass, and each is coloured black and yellow with double cones on the top. These marks indicate where the safest water lies, and which side of the danger or obstruction you should pass. For example, a vessel must pass to the north of a north cardinal mark, and to the west of a west cardinal mark.

At night, the lights on cardinal marks can be remembered by thinking of the compass rose as a clock: east (3 o'clock) 3 flashes; south (6 o'clock, 6 flashes and 1 long flash; west (9 o'clock)

0 flashes; north (12 o'clock) 12 continuous flashes. All cardinal marks have white light.

Note: A danger might not necessarily be surrounded by all four cardinal marks. It may also be designated by lateral marks where appropriate.

isolated danger marks

An isolated danger mark is a mark on an isolated danger which has water all around it.

signal flags

As most boats operate in the same area as manoeuvring ships and fishing boats, it is important to be able to decipher flag code signals other vessels my be displaying.

Today, one of the most important flags to be aware of is the one that indicates that a diver is working. If you see this flag slow down and keep well clear. Another flag to watch for is Flag T (red, white and blue), which signals the vessel is pair trawling; beware of the net being trawled between the two boats. (See inside cover for description of flags.)

Port-hand marks

Starboard hand marks

Shape: can, pillar or spar
Colour: red
Topmark (if any): red can
Light (if any): red, any rhythm other than preferred chanel

Shape: conical, pillar or spar
Colour: green
Top mark (if any): green cone
Light (if any): green, any rhythm other than preferred chanel

Isolated danger marks

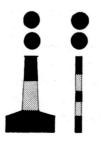

Shape: optional, but not conflicting with lateral, can or conical; pillar or spar preferred
Colour: black with one or more broad horizontal red bands
Topmark (if any): 2 black spheres, one above the other
Light (if any): white group, flashing F1(2)

Cardinal marks

ships manoeuvring by horns or sirens
manoeuvring and warning signals (*rule 34*)

One hoot:	I am turning to starboard
Two hoots:	I am turning to port.
Three hoots:	I am going astern.
A series of short hoots:	Get out of my way.

restricted visibility (*rule 35*)

In fog — thankfully a rare occurrence in New Zealand — vessels must use the following sound signals to indicate their intentions.

One prolonged blast at intervals of not more than two minutes
I am making way through the water under power.

Two prolonged blasts at intervals of not more than two minutes
I have stopped and am not making way through the water.

Bell rung rapidly for 5 seconds at intervals of not more than a minute
I am at anchor.

One prolonged blast followed by two short blasts at intervals of not more than two minutes
I am making way through the water under sail.

Note: A long blast on the horn is between 4–6 seconds and a short blast is only 1 second long.

distress signals

The following signals indicate distress and need of assistance:

- A gun fired at intervals of 1 minute.
- Rockets or shells throwing red stars at short intervals.
- The Morse code signal SOS (...– – –...).
- A 'mayday' signal sent by telephone.
- Flying of the flags N over C from the International Code of Signals.
- A square flag with a ball above or below it.
- Flames on a vessel as from burning tar or oil.
- A rocket parachute flare showing a red light.
- An orange-coloured smoke signal.
- Raising and lowering of arms repeatedly.
- The radio telegraph alarm signal.
- The radio telegraph alarm signal — a warbling sound signal.
- Signals from an emergency position indicating radio beacon.
- A piece of orange coloured canvas with appropriate signal for identification from the air.
- A dye marker.

TIPS ABOUT BOATING SAFETY

1. Check the boat, engine and equipment before leaving.
2. Check the weather forecast and tides before leaving.
3. Tell someone where you're going, and when you'll return.
4. Know the: Collision Prevention Rule, Water Recreation Rule, local bylaws.
5. Never overload the boat.
6. Take a proper lifejacket for each person on board; wear them.
7. Have aboard: Anchor, bailer, spare fuel, torch, warm gear.
8. Guard against fire.
9. Avoid alcohol when boating.
10. Take two means of communication: VHF, Flares, EPIRB, cellphone in a plastic bag.

Vessels overtaking: Every overtaking boat gives way (this includes sailing boats).

Power vessels head on: Both alter to starboard.

Power vessels crossing: Power boats give way to others on their starboard (right) side.

- Give way boats should cross behind.
- Always make a bold alteration as early as possible.
- Keep 50 metres apart if speed is over 5 knots.
- Sailing boats have different rules.

BE A RESPONSIBLE SKIPPER; DO A SAFE BOATING COURSE.

Maritime Safety

MARITIME SAFETY AUTHORITY OF NEW ZEALAND
Te Mana Ārai Hauata Moana o Aotearoa

Part 4 anchoring

drag

If your anchor is dragging it is probably because there is insufficient chain or warp. You need to let out more warp. Check for dragging by sighting along a transit. This is done by selecting a local feature, such as a tree or rock, that can be aligned with a more distant feature. If they stay in line, the craft is stationary. If the near feature appears to move forward in relation to the distant sighting, then the anchor is dragging.

drift

If anchoring near other boats, always check the likely swing patterns caused by tide or wind changes and allow sufficient room to manoeuvre when you decide to leave. Yachts with keels generally lie well to the wind because their centre of gravity is so low. However, trailer sailers, light displacement launches and other vessels with a lot of windage caused by high topsides and cabin tops will swing their anchors continually. At night in summer the wind may die right away, and drifting boats may cause problems and arguments.

Generally, excessive drifting can be corrected by taking in more warp. If overnighting in a bay, always check your anchor before retiring.

If you are alone aboard a yacht and it starts to drag ashore, just put the motor into slow ahead and motor out of danger with the anchor and warp still down.

hauling up the anchor

To haul up the anchor, motor forward very slowly in the direction of the warp. It is important that the person assigned to pull up the anchor does so quickly as the person steering the boat will have a lot of difficulty holding the boat's heading if the anchor is slow in coming up once it has broken from the seabed. Unfortunately, pulling up the anchor requires sheer brute strength and the stronger members of your crew should always do that task. Once the boat gains momentum it is much easier.

Difficulties with anchoring are often caused by lack of planning and communication, resulting in a shouting match between the crew. This is just bad seamanship. Learn to talk about your anchoring manoeuvre with other crew members before you begin, making sure everyone knows what they are to do.

fouling

If the anchor will not come up, it has fouled and has probably become snagged on some object or crevice on the seabed. First, try motoring slowly over the top of the anchor, with the warp cleated, and pull from the other direction. If this fails, motor around in a circle with a tight long warp, first in one direction and then the other. If all fails, tie the end of the warp to a buoy so that you can retrieve it later.

Note: You must be very careful not to pick up a cable with your anchor. If you think you have drifted with the tide and have anchored close to a cable, buoy your anchor warp and get help.

Part 5 chartwork

charts

Charts are produced by the Hydrographic Office of the Royal New Zealand Navy and are available from either the Office or from marine outlets.

Always carry a chart of the area in which your are sailing, and study it thoroughly. All charts show, as well as the general appearance of the coast and landforms, information about the depth of water, the type of sea bottom, buoys, lighthouses, tidal streams and currents. When buying your first charts, also purchase a copy of the *Chart Catalogue and Index*. This explains all the symbols and abbreviations found on the chart. Another publication, *The Coastal Cruising Handbook*, published by the Royal Akarana Yacht Club, is a valuable guide to coastal waters from North Cape to East Cape.

Note: The advice given in this chapter is only an introduction to navigation. If you are contemplating anything other than day trips close to the coast, you should complete a course in navigation.

soundings

On modern charts, the depth of water or sounding is shown in metres, below 31 metres it may be shown in metres and decimetres. On older charts soundings are shown in fathoms and in areas of less than 11 fathoms, fathoms and feet. (1 fathom = 6 feet.)

tides

All soundings shown on charts are calculated as the depth of water at low tide. Obviously, you will need to calculate for this when reading a chart, and this should be done by referring to the *New Zealand Nautical Almanac*. This contains a general description of tides and tidal streams, tidal definitions and a timetable of tides. This book also enables you to calculate the times and heights of tides in any place in New Zealand. Most daily newspapers also contain some basic tide information but not enough for tidal streams.

tidal streams

The direction and rate of tidal streams are marked on most charts. They are very important around estuaries, bars and channels where the difference between high and low water will result in vastly different sea conditions that can be dangerous. Be careful when sailing in areas where there is a strong tidal rip or current, and always check the effect of the weather and calculate how the tidal stream or rip is influencing your boat speed and direction (see following illustration).

Calculating tidal streams is best done on a chart. Almost all charts have one or more tidal lozenges — a lettered position shown in magenta with a corresponding reference table.

latitude and longitude

For navigation purposes the world is divided by a grid made from converging lines of latitude and longitude. The lines that run North and South are called the meridians of longitude. The first meridian runs through Greenwich, London, and this is where the measurements begin. With Greenwich as 0°, the world is divided into 360 meridians of longitude. These lines move West until 180° and then East counting down from 180 until they reach Greenwich again.

Latitude are the lines that run horizontally around the world, parallel to the equator. They are divided into North and South. Parts of degrees of latitude and longitude are always given in minutes.

distance

There is no scale of distance on marine charts for kilometres or land miles. Instead, distance is always measured on the latitude scale. One minute of latitude = 1 nautical mile. Sixty nautical miles = 1 degree of latitude. You measure distance by opening a pair of dividers between two points on the chart and transferring them to your latitude scale, always opposite to your position on the chart. Never measure distance by the longitude scale.

the compass rose

Most local charts carry two printed compass roses or circles marked off into 360°. The outer circle shows true north — the direction to which the chart is oriented — and the inner circle shows magnetic north (M). Information on magnetic variation is printed across the middle of the two roses.

The compass rose is present on all New Zealand coastal charts, but shows different magnetic variations according to area. This is printed across the middle of the two roses. (The further south of the equator you go, the greater the variation.)

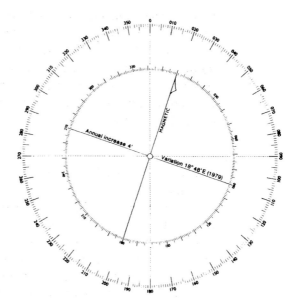

compasses

All boats, no matter what size, should carry a hand-bearing compass. This will allow you to take a bearing of a land object in order to fix your position. The compass is held horizontally, and the object sighted across the sights.

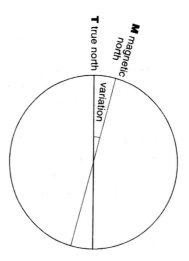

The difference between magnetic, true and compass north, and the effects of variation and deviation.

Larger boats with cabins should also carry a boat's compass. Situated close to the main steering station, the steering compass in one of the boat's most vital instruments. It should be gimbaled so that it may be read accurately at sea; the figures should also be large enough to be read by the helmsperson, and have a light for reading at night. When not in use the compass should be kept covered and out of the sun.

variation
The earth's magnetic field is constantly changing and the poles constantly moving. This rate of change in the position of magnetic north relative to New Zealand is about 3' each year, an increase so negligible that if you are using a modern chart you can entirely forget about it. (You can understand how really insignificant this increase is when you consider that very few people can steer within 3° of their course and there are 60' to a degree.)

Although charts are orientated to true north, there is no need to use true north for the vast majority of boating you are likely to do. Use magnetic north instead. Your compass points to magnetic north, you always steer to a magnetic course and the inner compass rose on a chart is oriented to magnetic north. If you want to use true north, you will need to subtract the magnetic variation — which involves unnecessary calculations.

log
Your log measures distance travelled through the water.

plotting a course
Use the following measurements as a guideline for how long your trip will take:

- 5 nautical miles at 5 knots will take 1 hour
- 2 1/2 nautical miles at 5 knots will take 1/2 an hour
- 1 nautical mile at 1 knot will take 1 hour
  (Divide boat speed into distance)

Global Positioning System (GPS)
The Global Positioning System is an excellent and reliable tool for anyone to use aboard boats of any size. I believe if you spend $10,000 on a boat you should have GPS aboard. Generally, the systems are available from $350 upwards. The GPS will give you a latitude and longitude position of where you are. It collects information form one of several satellites accounting for tide and

leeway and tells you exactly where you are. However, it is then important for you to be able to transfer this information to the chart that you are using, so you can see where you are in relation to rocks or islands.

The system can also give you a course to your destination, providing time and distance, how far along you are and other information that will make your voyage more enjoyable.

When plotting a position from your GPS to your chart, always check your counting of the latitude spaces. Do it twice is a good rule of thumb, remembering that all charts are of a different scale, given in gradients of 1, 5 or 10 miles, depending on the chart you have of the area you are in. Always calculate latitude before longitude. Your answer will be x degree, x minutes and x amount of points of a minute.

When you buy your GPS the operation manual will give very good detail of how to use the system to its full capability. The systems can either be battery or ship's power operated.

Part 6 the weather

More than any other factor, your safety at sea depends on the prevailing weather and tide conditions. Many accidents that occur at sea can be prevented if those concerned, before setting out, spend a few minutes checking the existing weather and sea conditions. Check the weather conditions before you go out and monitor the weather constantly while at sea. If the forecast is bad, stay at home; if you are already at sea and the weather deteriorates, find shelter or return home. If you decide to return home, never underestimate how quickly the weather can deteriorate — even in apparently fine weather, storms or squalls can arise, so at the first sign of threatening weather seek shelter. Above all, know the limits of your experience and capabilities of your craft.

marine forecasts

Before setting out you should check the marine forecasts for your area. It is important to obtain marine forecasts since forecasts for land areas are generally not applicable to sea conditions.

A great deal of weather forecast information is available to sailors to provide them with a knowledge of future weather conditions and to update the situation day-by-day. Newspapers, radio and television all provide weather information and special marine forecasts can be heard on national and local radio station. If you have a radio-telephone, forecasts are also broadcast on regional R/T services.

As well, a 24-hour recorded telephone marine forecast is available in Auckland, Wellington and Christchurch. The phone number is 0900-999- plus your area code.

Bear in mind that any forecast may be at odds with the actual situation and that local features may affect the weather you are receiving: keep a weather eye out.

Coastal weather forecasts can be obtained from the MetPhone service operated by the Meteorological Service. Calls are charged for.

MetPhone Coastal numbers: dial 0900-999+your area code number

Recreational marine area	Phone number
Bay of Islands	0900-000-09
Auckland Marine	0900-000-99
Lake Rotorua	0900-999-18
Lake Taupo	0900-000-13

Kapiti Coast	0900-000-17
Wellington Marine	0900-000-22
Christchurch Marine	0900-999-44

For those with a fax aboard, the MetService also operates a fax service. Dial MetFax 0900-77-999 on any touch-tone phone, enter the item number required from the menu and then key in your fax number to receive printed forecasts, maps and even satellite pictures.

MetFax numbers: dial 0900-999, then enter the numbers below

Recreational marine area	*Phone number*
Bay of Islands	22 998
Auckland Marine	22 999
Lake Rotorua	11 774
Lake Taupo	11 776
Kapiti Coast	22 445
Wellington Marine	22 444
Christchurch Marine	22 333

A list of item numbers is available from the MetService helpline at 0800-500-669. For help with either MetPhone or MetFax, call 0800-500-669.

Detailed information regarding weather broadcasts (New Zealand coastal broadcasts and storm warnings) is given in the *New Zealand Nautical Almanac*.

radio marine forecasts

Radio New Zealand broadcasts detailed marine forecasts. Your local commercial station will also often broadcast marine forecasts immediately after the local weather forecast at the end of the hourly news bulletin. Take a radio with you so that you can keep track of weather developments as they are updated in forecasts throughout the day.

Refer to the *Nautical Almanac* for frequencies of local coastal stations and their broadcast times of maritime forecasts. (You should purchase the updated edition of the *Almanac* each year.)

For those with VHF receivers, see the *Nautical Almanac* for the frequencies and broadcast times of local coastal radio forecasts.

The weather forecasts give the expected general conditions over a given forecast area — local modifications and conditions are not included. New Zealand has been divided into forecast areas and these extend about 60 nautical miles offshore with their boundaries located where the weather conditions often tend to change. Because the forecasts describe only general conditions and trends, it is useful to listen to the forecast for the zones next to the zone you are in as well as your own.

sources of marine forecasts for VHF radio

marine VHF radio		
where	**when**	**how**
VHF Ch 16	**0533, 0733, 1033, 1333, 1733, 2133**	**Listen on Channel 16 for a weather forecast announcement which will direct you to the channel for your area. (Ch 67, 68 or 71)**
VHF Ch 20, 21	**Continuous**	**Auckland area only**
VHF Ch 23	**Continuous**	**Whitianga area only**

forecast information
The forecasters' descriptions of wind conditions have particular meanings and are based on the Beaufort Scale, which describes wind conditions, on a scale of 0 to 12, starting with 0 (flat, calm) and rising to Force 12 (hurricane conditions).

Beaufort Scale

Scale Number	Description	Speed (9 km/h)	Characteristics
0	Calm	1	Smoke rises vertically
1	Light air	1–5	Smoke blown by wind
2	Light breeze	6–12	Leaves rustle
3	Gentle breeze	13–20	Extends a light flag
4	Moderate breeze	21–29	Raises dust and loose paper
5	Fresh breeze	30–39	Small trees sway
6	Strong breeze	40–50	Umbrellas difficult to use
7	Moderate gale	51–61	Difficult to walk
8	Fresh gale	62–74	Twigs snap from trees
9	Strong gale	75–87	Slates and chimneys blown away
10	Whole gale	88–102	Trees uprooted
11	Storm	103–120	Cars overturned, trees blown away
12	Hurricane	120+	Buildings destroyed

wind speed

One of the most important indicators of weather conditions is the wind speed. In forecasts, wind speeds are calculated as the mean or average speed over several minutes. However, winds can be expected to exceed the mean speed by as much as 50 percent, and in very gusty conditions close to headlands or steep terrain winds can increase to twice the mean speed forecast.

- A *strong wind* warning means gusts are expected to exceed 33 knots.
- A *gale* warning means average wind speed is expected to exceed 33 knots.
- A *storm* warning means average wind speed is expected to exceed 47 knots.
- A *squall* warning means showers may be accompanied by sudden but brief gales.

In some offshore areas, hazardous winds can suddenly occur without any warning being issued. Fouveaux and Cook straits, the South Taranaki Bight, Puysegur Point and the Otago coast are areas where this is most likely to happen.

visibility

Marine forecasts also give an indication of visibility and predict the likely reduction in showers or rain. Visibility describes the distance you can see in the given conditions.

Fair means a visibility of 3 to 6 nautical miles
Poor means a visibility of 1 to 3 nautical miles
Foggy means visibility of less than 1 nautical mile

wave heights

Wave heights are described as:

Calm	0 metres
Smooth	0.1 to 0.5 metres
Slight	0.5 to 1.25 metres
Moderate	1.25 to 2.5 metres
Rough	2.5 to 4 metres
Very rough	4 to 6 metres
High	6 to 9 metres
Very high	9 to 14 metres
Phenomenal	over 14 metres

Swell conditions are also given, with a prediction of swell height and direction.

predicting the weather

Get a <u>marine</u> forecast before you go boating. TV forecasts are too general.

Because the Meteorological Service forecasts over a vast area, its overview of weather conditions is never comprehensive, and may even be at odds with what is actually happening. **Never take the marine forecasts as gospel**. Instead, learn to predict the weather patterns for yourself. Squalls and storms occur suddenly and unless you are aware of the warning signs, your life can be in danger.

The weather in New Zealand is part of a global pattern generated by the heating and cooling of the earth as a whole. Warm air from the equator eventually meets cold, dense air flowing from the poles. At the same time, a force known as the Coriolis Force, generated by the earth's rotation, deflects this flowing air, producing the characteristic wind patterns of the world. In the New Zealand region, the prevailing winds are generally westerly, increasing in constancy and strength towards the south.

Amid these overall wind patterns, local changes and circulation occur. These result from differences in the atmospheric pressure. Where air is rising, air pressure is lowered; where is it descending, air pressure is increased. This produces the pattern of high- and low-pressure systems so characteristic of New Zealand's weather.

Atmospheric pressure itself is now measured in hectapascals (formerly millibars) and the lines joining points of equal pressure are termed isobars, which, like the contours of a hill or valley on a map, radiate from areas of high or low pressure. (These are the lines depicted on forecast maps.)

what do the forecast words mean?

- *Situation* is the key information on today's weather map such as highs, lows and fronts.
- *Forecasts*: these predict the most likely outcome, but the situation helps you ascertain the alternatives.

wind

Wind is always described by:
- The direction it blows from, for example, north-west.
- Its speed in knots (nautical miles per hour).
- Wind measurement should always be taken to mean the speed,

plus or minus 5 knots. If the forecast is for north-west winds, 15 knots, you can safely assume the direction will vary between northerly and westerly and the speed will be from 10 to 20 knots.

• Land contour can affect the direction of the breeze and halve or double its speed.

• Wind at sea can gust to a speed of half-again-more-than-the-average. A 20 knot average wind can gust to 30 knots.

depressions, troughs and fronts

Systems of low pressure are usually called *depressions*. Here, winds converge towards the centre of the depression at sea level, and rise up out of the system, extending thousands of metres vertically in to the atmosphere. Associated with them are strong winds, extensive cloud and rain. Depressions are described as shallow, moderate or intense, according to the value of the central pressure — 1000 hp would be shallow, 970 hp intense. Normally, the deeper or more intense the depression, the more active the conditions — stronger winds, more extensive cloud and rain, and so on. Sometimes even shallow depressions may bring active weather conditions and skippers should view with caution any depression in the northern latitudes of New Zealand because these can be both shallow and active.

In the Southern Hemisphere, winds circulate around a depression in a clockwise direction. This has given rise to a rule, known as the Boy-Ballot's Law, which enables the mariner to determine the position of the depression's centre. (It is not useful on land where local features and topography may affect the wind flow.)

to determine the position of a depression centre

1. Stand directly facing the wind.
2. Extend your left arm from your side so that it is a bit more than a right angle (110°) from the wind or 2 points aft of the beam.
3. The centre of the depression will lie in the direction that your left arm is pointing.

By constantly monitoring the position of the centre over several hours and by determining whether the wind has increased in strength or not, you can tell whether the depression is approaching or passing away from you. If the bearing remains constant (that is, the left hand points in the same direction), and the wind strength is increasing, it is likely that the depression centre is moving towards you. Conversely, a constant bearing and decreasing winds suggest that the centre is moving away.

Associated with depressions are troughs, which are V- or U-shaped extensions from a depression centre. A feature known as a front often lies within these troughs. Like depressions, they are associated with strong winds, extensive cloud and rain. The passage of troughs and fronts across New Zealand, usually extending from a depression passing to the south, is more common than an actual depression centre crossing the country.

The best way of determining the passage and intensity of a depression or trough is by using a *barometer*. Barometers measure atmospheric pressure. The approach of a depression or trough is shown by falling pressure. The deeper the depression, or the faster its approach, the faster the pressure will fall. A drop of only 3 hectapascals in three hours represents a rapid fall.

Barometers vary considerably in accuracy and cost. Despite the cost, barometers are a useful piece of equipment for the skipper who can keep one either at home or on board.

anticyclones

High-pressure systems are usually called *anticyclones*. Like depressions, they extend thousands of metres vertically, but with anticyclones air currents converge aloft, flow down and out at the surface. They usually bring settled, fine weather and light winds. Normally they are large in area, slow moving and, unlike depressions, wind circulates around them in an anti-clockwise direction. They are described as weak, moderate or intense according to the value of the central system. 1010 hp is considered weak, 1030 hp intense. Generally, the more intense an anticyclone, the more prolonged the fair weather it brings.

An associated feature of anticyclones is the ridge of high pressure. Like the anticyclone, it also brings fair weather but it can also be accompanied by strong winds, especially when an advancing ridge is rapidly following a low-pressure system. When air pressure raises rapidly, it is commonly accompanied by an increase in wind strength — usually lasting 24 hours before abating.

weather warnings

Always keep a careful eye out for the weather. In particular, watch for these conditions:

cirrus clouds

High, delicately defined clouds that appear as strands, patches or as a thin sheet. These are a characteristic feature of depressions which form north of New Zealand. Expect a change for the worse, usually within 24 to 48 hours.

cumulus clouds

These clouds, with their familiar cotton-wool shape, are a sign of unstable conditions. Expect wind gusts.

cumulonimbus clouds

These are larger towering clouds building high in the sky and are a sign of thunderstorms. **Beware.** Although there might be gentle, steady winds blowing towards the storm clouds, severe and sudden squalls may strike from the opposite direction.

fast-moving, low clouds

The appearance of these clouds precedes a sharp increase in wind speed.

wind change

Any wind change, especially when cumulus and cumulonimbus clouds are present, is a warning that squalls or gusts are about to strike.

local coastal conditions

Coastal weather conditions have their own characteristics. Wind travels a lot faster over the sea than over the land — often twice as fast. However, when wind strikes a cape or headland, or is channelled by a strait or sound, wind speed is further increased — often to three times that experienced in a nearby sheltered bay.

Never be lulled into a false sense of security by sheltering at the lee of a steep terrain. Gusts and squalls can still sweep over the land and strike you suddenly.

typical sea weather

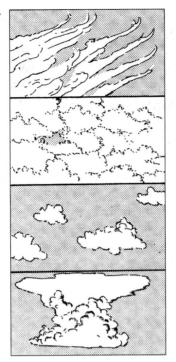

Wind: north-north-west, 10 knots
Cloud: cirrus
Conditions: fair to fine but a change likely to south-west with rain

Wind: light to moderate, variable, north-north-east
Cloud: stratocumulus
Conditions: fair with morning drizzle

Wind: variable winds, sea breezes
Cloud: cumulus
Conditions: clear skies, fair weather

Wind: westerly, 20–30 knots
Cloud: large cumulonimbus
Conditions: heavy rain

how to fine tune the forecast

To get the best from the forecast, apply your own local knowledge, then you will be able to predict wind direction and strength as it is most likely to affect YOU.

Look on a weather forecast as being a smoothed-out ideas that needs to be fine-tuned to your location. Do this with an eye on the sky, another on the barometer, and a knowledge of the local land forms, tides and currents.

This will help you adjust the generalised forecast back to the piece of the real world you are boating in.

Map and some text contribution kindly provided by the Maritime Safety Authority of New Zealand Te Mana Arai Hauata Moana o Aotearoa.

Part 7 boating in bad weather

boating under motor

Always head into the waves at a slight angle if you are in difficult sea conditions. It will be more comfortable, drier and safer to steer first on one side of the waves and then after a period turn the boat through the wind and steer on the other side so you are criss-crossing your track. If you are experiencing some bigger seas rolling up in front of you, pull the boat off so you meet these at an angle of approximately 30°. If you turn too far away from it you are likely to have the sea break aboard, but at 30° the wave will strike the boat forward of the beam, lessening the impact. If you are experiencing difficult head-to-sea conditions for your boat, don't drive at high speeds into the waves and wind. The pounding will make the boat unmanageable and you are likely to cause damage and injury because of violent motion.

If running with the wind and waves, don't wave-ride or you may broach. (Your boat will swing beam into the waves, causing her to be swamped.) Keep your speed under control so that you don't ride to the top of the wave but stay about one-third of the way up. When the wave you are on breaks, move forward to the next, positioning your boat as before.

Rather than steering directly downwind, steer at a slight angle so the seas approach your boat on the quarter.

under sail

As the wind increases, you should first reduce your sail area by reefing or changing to a smaller sail. All yachts must carry a storm jib. Too many yachts get into early difficulties in a blow and suffer bad gear damage because the crew has been too slow in taking off sail.

A yacht's greatest danger is the lee shore. Always try to make for shelter to windward. Take into account how you approach the waves. Don't sail too close to the wind. Bear off so you can take the sea just forward of the beam. When there is a lull you may be able to point a little higher.

Downwind, the same applies as for a boat under power.

In bad weather you may sometimes feel that you can no longer cope and wish only to heave to. This is only one option, however, and although it will give you a short respite it does mean that you lose full control over your craft. The wind and tide will still be buffeting you and close to the coast this could be dangerous. If possible, keep going. However, if you must rest and heave to, then the procedure that you follow will be determined by the prevailing conditions.

In moderate to light conditions, sail on a tight reach, that is, wind just forward of beam and let out your sails so that they flap. This may be suitable for short stops but the flapping sails will strain the sails and rigging.

For longer stops and in heavier winds, back the headsail, lash the tiller to leeward and ease out the mainsail. In very strong winds lower one of the sails, normally the mainsail. However, each yacht is slightly different and some experimenting is required.

sea anchors

These can sometimes be used to slow the boat's progress in storm conditions. A drogue or sea anchor is an open-ended conical canvas bag attached to a rope and trailed from the boat from either the stern or bow. Rubber tyres or even a chilly bin attached to the end of a rope can also be used as sea anchors.

Those planning extended voyages or offshore racing should read K. Adlard Cole's book, *Heavy Weather Sailing*, which is regarded worldwide as the definitive work on survival at sea in extreme conditions.

SECTION 2
emergencies

Part 8 in an emergency

Good boathandling is about anticipating and reacting effectively to every eventuality. Nowhere is this more evident than with man overboard drills — what to do if someone falls overboard. Your skills here may mean the difference between someone drowning or surviving. If they hit their head when they fall and are unconscious in the water, every second you take to retrieve them will be vital. Practise your drill repeatedly, and if you have a regular crew, make sure each crew member knows the procedure you will follow. Children should also know the drill and be able to help in all aspects of it. Pan and Mayday signals should be adhered to in all emergency situations.

Remember that prevention is better than cure. Always ensure that safety lines are rigged, and safety harnesses are worn by all people on deck when the weather is rough and at night.

man overboard drill

'Man overboard'
As soon as you notice that someone has fallen overboard call out 'Man overboard' to alert the other crew member/s.

Stop the boat as quickly as possible
Remember the visible portion of someone who has fallen into the water is immediately reduced to their head and perhaps a waving arm, which will rapidly diminish if you continue to pull away. Visibility is worse at night or in heavy weather.

The quickest method to stop a yacht is to gybe immediately and let all sheets go. No matter what point of sailing you are on, no matter what part of the yacht the person has fallen over, gybe. You will go around quickly and finish alongside the person in the water. Alternatively, you could luff your boat up into the wind, drop your sails and motor back. Yet another method is to reach-tack-reach with the engine running.

In powerboats take the power off immediately — the whirling propeller blades are a potential hazard. As you take the power off, turn the boat away from the wind.

Man overboard — the gybe manoeuvre.

If you are sailing or boating short-handed, don't waste time throwing out a life buoy (probably in the wrong place). Just get the boat stopped and turned around by gybing, then throw your buoys into the water.

Approach from leeward
Always approach the person in the water coming up into the wind from the leeward side. Under no circumstances come down on them from windward. You have no control, the person will be drifting away from you and you could run them down.

Haul the person aboard
If the person is conscious, young and strong enough, it should be easy to get them up a ladder or up a rope. However, if they are elderly, unfit or unconscious, you will have to get a rope around them. Tie a bowline with a big loop in it and, having brought them alongside with a boat hook, pass the loop over their head and get it around their chest and under their arms. Throw the free end over the boom. You may need to tie the boom out board then take it around a winch. Winch the person up and out of the water. If you are short-handed you may have to get into the water yourself. Remember to tie a bowline around yourself and tie it tightly to a secure point on board. Make sure you are able to get on board again.

fire
Fire on board is one of the great potential hazards of boating so, no matter what size or type your boat, you should always have a fire extinguisher on board. Make sure that it is regularly serviced, stored

in an accessible place, and that all crew members know how to use it.

A common misconception is that leaking petrol evaporates entirely. It doesn't. Petrol vapour is heavier than air and tends to collect in spaces like the bilge. Mixed with air it is potentially explosive and can be ignited by one small spark, like that created when you turn on the starter motor. If you smell petrol treat it with extreme caution. Don't turn anything on, instead, get air flowing through the boat and bilges.

Liquefied gas should also be treated with care. Like petrol fumes, it is heavier than air and if it has leaked it will settle in the bilges where it can be ignited by a small spark. Because liquefied gas does not smell, a gas detector alarm is a worthwhile investment. They are not expensive and can be bought from most marine outlets and gas distributors.

Diesel fuel and vapour will also cause fire, although generally it is a much safer fuel than petrol.

precautions

Regularly check all fuel and stove leads and pipes by applying a thick solution of soapy water to all connections. If it bubbles, you have a leak.

Store gas cylinders away from the galley, preferably in the cockpit. Alternatively, build a gas bottle locker that is airtight and drains over the side. Make a rule of not letting anyone smoke below deck.

fire extinguishers

The most effective fire extinguishers are those using CO_2 dry power. The CO_2 smothers the fire, starving it of oxygen. With fuel or gas fires, water may merely spread the fire. However, a woollen blanket soaked in water is an effective way of smothering a fire. When fighting a fire, act quickly, get close and aim low.

towing

If you lose power and require assistance, it is likely you will have to accept a tow.

You will need a long rope. If you have to extend it with another length, the easiest way is to join the two together with a bowline. Make sure that your towing warp does not go around corners otherwise it will chafe. Also, when being towed, keep the line tensioned. Don't attach the line to just one cleat; you will need to rig a towing bridle with the line taking the strain evenly on at least three strong points, such as the mast and two deck cleats. The actual towing line from these three points needs to be central and in very rough conditions when steerage is difficult, towing a rope or chain from the stern may help control the boat.

sinking

If your boat is holed or begins to take water from a swamping, or capsizes, swift action needs to be taken. Every vessel will behave differently in these circumstances but so much will depend on the conditions at the time — the size of your boat, how quickly critical buoyancy is lost and whether action can be taken to reduce or regain it.

Like all other things in boating your survival and ability to cope with an emergency will depend on how well you have planned for your voyage, no matter how short it may be. No trip should be made in any boat without lifejackets for all members of the crew and guests. Each person should be designated their own lifejacket at the beginning of the voyage when they should be fitted and adjusted. In emergencies lifejackets should be worn. On extended voyages wear safety harnesses.

Your vessel, no matter how small, should have adequate bailing equipment that should include a hand bilge pump and buckets. Having only an electric-operated bilge pump is unwise. In survival conditions, even close to shore, you may well have no power yet need to clear water quickly and in volume from the boat.

If you are in need of assistance your should let off a flare and send a Mayday call on your VHF and single sideband radio (*see pages 164–167*). The procedures should be displayed next to your radio so that everyone, even a passenger without boating experience, can see how to send a distress message.

Small vessels, like runabouts, can sink very rapidly if the vessel has not got adequate buoyancy. Carry as much as you can on board or under the seats — it could well save your life.

abandoning boat

Although this depends very much on the conditions, always remember that it is preferable to stay with your vessel for as long as possible.

You will be surprised at its buoyancy even with a lot of water aboard. In the English Fastnet yacht race in 1979, a fierce storm resulted in loss of life. Many crews abandoned their vessels too quickly. The next day, when the storm had passed, the yachts were found still floating and in sound condition. Unfortunately, many crew members had either drowned or died of exposure. Your lame vessel, if it is afloat, will give you better protection.

life rafts

If you have a large vessel and like taking extended coastal cruises in open water or offshore voyages, you should purchase one of the approved brands of life raft. These can be stowed on deck. In an emergency the life raft is dropped into the water. Once in the water the inflation cord is pulled and the raft will inflate in approximately 30 seconds.

On board the raft there should be a survival kit catering for minimum needs: water, torch, repair kit, paddles, bellows, bailer, fishing line, first aid kit and sea anchor. You should supplement this with your own kit.

There have been some amazing stories about people surviving in life rafts. Possibly the most remarkable is the story of Steven Callahan. His book, *Adrift*, is recommended reading for all who wish to go offshore. Callahan survived 76 days adrift with a combination of some good fortune, courage, tenacity and good planning. He took into the life raft with him a specially prepared survival bag that was handily placed near the cockpit of his boat. In it was an assortment of survival equipment that saved his life.

radio distress procedures
radio distress calling
Procedures for distress calls are the same for both SSB and VHF.

Emergency means 'a vessel or a person is in grave and imminent danger and requires immediate assistance.' When you have an emergency do the following:

Switch to 2182 kHz or 156.8MHz (channel 16) or 4125 kHz — the international distress frequencies (any other frequency may be used if it is known that the nearest station or ship is keeping watch on that frequency).

1. Alarm signal (where possible), say 'MAYDAY MAYDAY MAYDAY'.
   Say 'This is (vessel name and call sign)' 3 times.
   Give the three P's
   (i)   The vessel's POSITION (use either latitude and longitude, or a bearing and distance off a well-known geographical feature).
   (ii) The PROBLEM — a quick description of the distress, for example, fire, man overboard and so on.
   (iii) The number of PEOPLE on board.
2. State the nature of help required.

3. Give any other information which may assist rescue.
4. Listen on the same frequency for acknowledgement.
5. If any other ship interrupts, say: 'SEELONCE, MAYDAY'.
6. If there is no reply, be prepared to repeat the message.

Urgency means you need assistance but life is not at risk. Use 'PAN PAN'.

1. Switch to 2182kHz or 156.8MHz (channel 16), the international distress frequencies. (Any other frequency may be used if it is known that the nearest station is keeping watch on that frequency.)
2. Say 'PAN PAN, PAN PAN, PAN PAN'.
3. Give the name of the station required 3 times.
4. Say 'This is (vessel name and call sign)' 3 times.
   Give the three P's
   (i)   The vessel's POSITION (use either latitude and longitude, or a bearing and distance off a well-known geographical feature).
   (ii)   The PROBLEM — a quick description of the distress, for example, fire, man overboard and so on.
   (iii)   The number of PEOPLE on board.
5. Listen on the same frequency for acknowledgement.

If your hear 'SECURITE' (say-cure-e-tay), this indicates that a navigational or meteorological warning is to follow.

Cancellation of distress or urgency calls and messages

Distress and urgency calls and messages must be cancelled if it is subsequently found that assistance is not required.

Example — MAYDAY

Say 'MAYDAY (once). All Stations (3 times). This is (name of vessel and call sign — 3 times). Cancel my earlier MAYDAY, help no longer required — out.'

Example — URGENCY

Say 'All stations (or a particular station — 3 times). This is (name of vessel and call sign — 3 times). Cancel my earlier URGENCY call. Engine now repaired — out.'
Unnecessary chatter should be avoided at all times.

If you hear a distress message
1. Listen carefully. If possible, write down the message and time.
2. Listen for acknowledgement from a coastal radio station.
3. If no acknowledgement is heard acknowledge, then resend the message.
4. Say 'MAYDAY RELAY' 3 times.
5. Say 'This is (vessel name and call sign)' 3 times.
6. Give distress message as sent by the vessel in distress.
7. Give assistance if possible. Advise station of what you are doing.
8. Continue to listen in.
9. If other radio traffic interrupts say 'SEELONCE, DISTRESS. This is (vessel name and call sign).'

flares and distress signals

Every vessel, no matter how small, should have on board distress flares. These should be stored in a dry place on board, and be regularly checked to ensure that they have not got damp or exceeded their expiry date. A miniflare pack can be purchased for a small outlay. It is well packed and includes eight rockets, a gun and instructions for use.

A more comprehensive set for vessels making longer passages should include:

Red-parachute rocket
Designed to reach over 300 metres and will burn for 40 seconds.
Red hand flare
Effective for pinpointing your position over a short range or in reduced visibility. It is hand-held and burns for 60 seconds. The red flare is the internationally recognised signal for distress.
Buoyant orange smoke
This signal burns for 3 minutes, with a dense cloud of orange smoke. It may be placed in the water and is ideal for alerting aircraft.
Hand-held orange flare
This burns for 40 seconds and is ideal for a clear day when a red hand flare may not be so readily visible to pinpoint your position.
Dye marker
A recognised distress signal that can be attached to a horse-shoe life raft.
White flare
Although this is not a distress signal, it could be used to alert

another vessel at night that it may be on a collision course with you when you have no other means of attracting its attention.

Emergency locator beacon (EPIRB)

When activated, this beacon sends a warbling radio signal out on the distress frequency that can be picked up and so pinpoint your position. Recommended for all vessels that undergo extended coastal or offshore voyages.

marine radio

A marine radio is essential for reporting emergency situations. Only use a cellphone if nothing else is available — use the radio first. VHF radio is heard by the coastguard and all other boaties in the area. Only use a cellphone if you **do not** have a radio at hand — call *500 in the Auckland area only and 111 elsewhere.

SECTION 3
equipment

safety equipment

Vessels under 4.6 metres (15 feet) should have:

> One lifejacket for each person
> Adequate anchor, warp and chain
> Pumping or bailing equipment
> A means of signalling

Vessels over 4.6 metres (15 feet) and under 6.1 metres (20 feet) should have in addition to the above a better means of signalling for help — for example, R/T, flares, mirror, markers and so on — and a fire extinguisher (if power driven or stove on board).

For all other vessels 6.1 metres (20 feet) and over — as above with the addition of:

> Lifebuoy
> First aid kit
> Rigid or inflatable dinghy
> Compass and local charts
> Flashlight

Vessels in this category are also recommended to carry:

> Alternative steering
> Anchors (1–2)
> Bilge pump
> Boat hook
> Buckets with lanyard
> Chain
> Charts
> Compass
> Deviation card
> Dinghy with buoyancy and bailer
> Dividers
> Fire extinguishers
> First aid kit and manual
> Flares (hand-held)
> Flares (parachute)
> Flashlight and batteries
> Fog horn
> Fresh water
> Guard rails

Hand-bearing compass
Life raft
Lifebuoys or heaving ring
Lifejackets
Lines or rope
Mobile phone*
Navigation lights
Parallel rule
Pilot book, nautical almanac
R/T schedules
Radar reflector
Radio-telephone
Safety harness
Shut-off valve on fuel
Smoke
Sounder or leadline
Spare or dual battery system
Tool kit
Warp (1–2)

Mobile phones are increasingly in use by boaties out for day trips around the coast. If you have a mobile phone, always take it with you. If you have a marine radio, use that first.

children aboard

All children on a boat must have their own lifejackets with a yoke that is comfortable to wear and correctly fitted. A flotation vest is also of great value and is excellent for children learning water skills. It will give them confidence in the water long before they have learnt to swim.

Never take a child in a small open boat, even for a short journey, without them wearing their lifejacket or vest.

Part 9 medical aid

No matter what size the boat, each boat should carry a medical kit. Even if you have a runabout and are going for a day's fishing, carry a basic kit with you. If your boat has a cabin, then the kit should be permanently stored aboard — updated, kept dry and checked regularly.

The medical kit listed below is basic and is not intended to cater for individual medical requirements. If there is any possibility that special medication is needed for any crew member, medical advice should be obtained before putting to sea.

medical kits
absorbent gauze
adhesive plaster, 25 mm x 5 mm
antihistamine tablets
antiseptic burn cream
antiseptic detergent, Dettol or similar
antiseptic wound cream, Savlon or similar
aspirin, Paracetamol or similar
bandage, crepe, 75 mm wide
bandages, triangular
bandages, white open wove, 50 mm wide
Bandaids or similar
calomine/antihistamine cream or lotion
cottonwool, 60 gm packs
first aid handbook (St John Ambulance Association manual
   recommended)
insect repellant
Lomotol (antidiarrheal)
sunblock cream
Marzine, Sealegs or similar
Non-adherent dressing
Optrex eye lotion
safety pins of rustless and stainless metal
scissors
self-adhesive sutures or butterfly clips
tweezers
waterproof spray bandage

seasickness

Nelson suffered from it and most people do at some time or other if they spend a lot of time at sea in a variety of conditions. It affects people in different ways but at its most severe it can be debilitating. Thankfully, for most people it passes and the body and balance soon become accustomed to the motion of the sea.

There are certain things you can do to help to prevent seasickness before going to sea. Don't eat rich or fatty foods and don't drink too heavily before you set off. Once at sea, keep your dry food intake up and liquid intake down. If, however, you feel queasy, lie down if you can.

There are a number of medicines on the market today that have proved helpful to sufferers. If you habitually suffer from seasickness, you should begin taking the medicine before departure. These include:

conventional travel sickness preparations: Avomine, Sealegs, Dramamine or Marzine. All are readily available without prescription. For a travel sickness preventative suitable for children, see your chemist.

seabands Worn on the wrist. These fit snugly around the wrists and apply pressure to the acupuncture points on your wrist.

vitamin B6: Certainly worth considering and is often suggested for pregnancy nausea with good results.

hypothermia

Hypothermia is caused by the lowering of the body's temperature as a result of exposure to cold. Beyond a critical temperature the body reacts by going into a coma. Death may result. It is not just brought on by being in water for a long period — estimated at 2 1/2 to 3 hours in New Zealand waters. Anyone not adequately clothed for cold weather and exposed for even a short time may develop symptoms.

symptoms of hypothermia
1. Intense shivering difficult to control, problems with speaking.
2. Shivering increases, no co-ordination, thinking muddled.
3. Muscles cease to function, pulse slows, unable to reason, breathing problems.
4. At its most extreme, the patient will become unconscious and have an erratic heartbeat.
5. Brain cells cease to function, heart and lungs fail.

treatment of hypothermia
1. Remove wet clothing immediately.
2. Wrap the patient in layers of warm, dry clothing.
2. If the patient is conscious, get them to drink a hot, sweet drink.
4. Never administer alcohol, under any circumstances.
5. Do not massage their limbs as it may take the heat away from the central body area.

Part 10 mechanical and electrical systems

At sea, if your engine breaks down or fails to start, you could be in serious difficulty. For that reason, it is essential you carry a viable alternative means of propulsion. If you have a runabout, then you should carry at least a pair of oars on board at all times; if you have a small launch with an inboard engine, then you should carry an outboard motor on the transom.

A working knowledge of the engine and the mechanics of your boat are also essential. A faulty seacock will soon swamp a boat unless you know what to do. Similarly, if your engine breaks down at sea, it will probably be you who has to fix it.

operation and maintenance

Before you set out you should have a sound working knowledge of how to operate and maintain all the equipment on the boat. What should you know about?

anchor winch
auxiliary equipment
batteries
bilge pumps
cooling system
emergency starting
engine mountings
fuel system and filters
fuel tanks and valves
fuses
gas system
gearbox
lubricating systems and filters
navigation, lights and instruments
seacocks
shaft bearings
starting and stopping procedure
steering system
water pumps

fuel systems

The rate of consumption on a boat is highly variable and is affected by the wind, sea and tides. If reserve supplies are limited, as they are on most small boats, you should always carefully monitor your fuel consumption and calculate for your return voyage.

petrol

Most outboard engines are two-stroke, requiring the engine lubricating oil to be mixed with the petrol at a specified ratio. Always adhere to the manufacturer's recommendations.

Because petrol is such a highly volatile spirit, be careful when fuelling and check for fuel leaks. (This is particularly important with inboard petrol engines.) A spark from the starter motor can easily ignite if it comes into contact with petrol vapour.

diesel

Diesel is far less volatile than petrol and consequently less dangerous to use in confined spaces, making it a safer fuel for inboard engines. Another advantage is that fuel consumption is substantially more economical than petrol.

These features have allowed engine manufacturers to develop relatively lightweight diesel engines with high specific outputs compared with engines a few years ago.

A common problem will all diesel engines is that fuel filters can become blocked very easily, resulting from the presence of fungi in the fuel system. This usually manifests itself as a slimy, brown fibrous substance. The fungi can only develop in the presence of water, which finds its way into fuel tanks through condensation. As the fuel in the tank gets used it is replaced by air, sometimes humid, and when conditions are right the moisture turns to water and falls to the bottom of the tank. In these conditions, fungi can grow.

The best way to clean out the system is to flush out the fuel lines and add a biocide that will kill the fungi. Many diesel fuel additives that improve engine performance also include a biocide agent. However, whenever a biocide is added to eliminate fungi, your filters will become blocked as the dead fungi is carried out of the system. The best way to prevent this is to add a biocide regularly.

tips for outboard motors

Before starting, ensure that the motor is securely fastened to the transom and that safety chains are fitted. Check the electrical system, that the spark plug is clean and correctly set, and that no leads are frayed. Check that the fuel switch cock is turned on, and that the air intake valve is open on the petrol tank. Ensure that the manufacturer's specified ratio of oil to petrol is followed.

Propellers must be regularly checked for wear or damage caused by striking objects. Any change in vibration or pitch should be immediately checked since a damaged or incorrectly balanced propeller can in turn damage shaft bearings and engine parts.

tips for inboard engines

If the ignition is electric, all leads should be well insulated and dry at all times. They should also not be placed where they may be exposed to fuel vapours. With all petrol engines, gas detectors and alarms should be installed and fire extinguishers located in accessible positions in the event of an emergency.

Drip trays should also be installed under the engine and fuel tanks, and exhaust pipes should be well secured and clear of all woodwork.

The battery should be placed in a wooden or polythene box, securely fastened as high as possible away from the bilges. The box should also be covered to prevent seaspray shorting the terminals or items falling on the battery and crossing the terminals. Regularly check the water level.

pre-trip checklist

Before setting out you should spend 5 to 10 minutes carrying out a few basic checks:

- Open doors, hatches, and so on, and ventilate the cabin for 5 to 10 minutes before starting any electrical appliance or the engines. If petrol or diesel fumes are present, check for leaks and air out the bilges.
- Check the overall condition of the engine, looking for anything that may have become loose or broken.
- Check that fuel lines are not chafed.
- Check oil levels.
- Open cooling water valves and check the water level.
- Check all belt drives on the engine.
- Check the electrolyte level in the battery and turn on the main isolating switch.
- Check that you have adequate fuel supplies for your trip and that the fuel is turned on at the tank or that the switch cock is 'on'. On engines where a fuel return is fitted, and where more than one tank has been installed, ensure that the fuel has been returned to the tank in service.
- If an exhaust cap is fitted, ensure it is removed.
- Operate the throttle and gearbox controls to ensure they operate and do not stick. You may need to lubricate all linkages and pins.

You can now start the engine. Check the instruments and confirm that all readings are correct. Next, check the cooling water flows overboard, and listen to the engine to satisfy yourself that all is well. You can now proceed with confidence on your planned trip.

if the engine does not start

petrol engines
Check that the petrol switch cock is open and that the air intake on the petrol tank is also open.

One of the main causes of engine failure in petrol engines is a fault in the high tension electrical ignition system. All electrical components must be kept dry. Also check that the leads are not wrongly connected and that the spark plugs or distributor points are clean. They may need cleaning or resetting.

If your engine stalls, first check that you are not idling too slowly or that the fuel mixture is not too rich. Failing that you will need to check your electrical system.

diesel
In diesel engines the main causes of engine failure are faulty fuel systems or cooling systems.

A faulty fuel system can usually be detected by the engine performance gradually fading away before total failure occurs. Apart from the problems associated with fungal contamination, a faulty fuel system may develop when air enters the system through faulty connections or seals.

A faulty cooling system, on the other hand, is usually detected by an increase in temperature indicated by engine instruments. When this happens act promptly lest your engine seizes. Begin by inspecting the overboard discharge to ensure that the cooling water flow is normal.

A faulty cooling system may result from blocked sea suction, faulty water pump, air in the system, a faulty thermostat, blocked cooling water spaces in the engine, a dirty heat exchanger, faulty suction or overboard discharge valves.

Breakdowns in diesel engines resulting from faulty electrical systems are usually confined to being unable to start the engine in the first place. This may be because of a flat battery or poor battery connections, broken or damaged wires, the glow plugs not working, fuel shut down, or a faulty starter motor.

Note: A sudden fall in engine performance could indicate a fouled propeller.

basic tools

Always carry enough tools to enable you to carry out repairs on board. Adjustable tools are convenient and if your craft is fitted with an inboard engine your tool kit should include the following: three sizes of screwdriver, a Phillips screwdriver, pump pliers, self-locking grip, a knife, ring and open-ended spanners, socket set, adjustable spanners, a medium-sized pipe wrench, a filter bowl wrench, a hacksaw and blades, a hammer and a torch.

spare parts

For inboard engines, whether diesel or petrol, you should always carry: primary and secondary fuel filters, a lube oil filter for the engine, a lube oil filter for the gear box, grease, CRC, 4 metres of electrical wire, rubber and multi-purpose joining material, pipe thread tape, gland packing, spare belts for drives, a fuel injector for diesel engines, spark plugs and a set of contact points for petrol engines.

For outboard motors you should carry: spark plugs, a set of contact points, insulating tape, propeller pin, CRC and grease.

Always take care of your spare parts and tools, and store them where they will keep dry. Also, remember to carry your service manual on board at all times.

SECTION 4
allied water sports

water skiing and jet skiing

Water skiing and jet skiing are subject to the Water Recreation Regulations. These specify that no person in charge of a boat towing a water skier or aquaplane board will exceed 5 knots within:

- 30 metres of another vessel or person in the water.
- 200 metres of the shore or any structure.
- 200 metres of a vessel or raft flying a diver-operating flag.

If an area has been set aside for water skiers it will be marked and speed restrictions will not be applicable within the reserved area.

At all times there must be a second person in a boat towing a water skier or aquaplane who continually watches the person being towed. The responsibility for this is shared between all parties, including the person being towed.

windsurfing

Under the regulations, windsurfers are deemed to be operating a small sailing craft, and therefore have the same legal responsibilities as any other operator of a sailing craft.

tips for windsurfers
- Novices should be aware of their limitations and the physical nature of the sport
- Always wear a buoyancy vest and wear clothing appropriate to the conditions, preferably a wetsuit.
- Don't swim away from your board to retrieve any gear. Stay with your board at all times.
- Until you are proficient, windsurf with others.
- Learn the correct signals to attract attention if you are in difficulty.
- Remember, a windsurfer moves across the water quickly and people piloting other vessels may not see you.

recipes

The following is a selection of tried and tasty recipes which are easy to prepare afloat.

Soup Plus

Dehydrated packet soups can be given a boost by first sautéing a sliced onion in the saucepan in a little butter. Make up the packet soup as usual on top of the onion. If you like, add a few freeze-dried peas as well. (Freeze-dried peas are good to add to all sorts of meals like stews, casseroles etc. Keep some in a jar handy to the stove.)

Fish Chowder

3 to 4 fish heads or fillets
1 onion, diced
¼ cup diced green pepper
1 clove garlic, minced
1 tbsp butter
1 tbsp oil
2 medium potatoes, diced
1 can tomatoes
1 stick celery, finely chopped
pinch of mixed herbs
1 tsp salt
¼ tsp black pepper
parsley, chopped

Simmer fish heads in 2 cups of water for about 15 minutes. Remove fish heads, reserving broth, and pick meat from the heads. Retain meat and throw away bones. Sauté onion, pepper and garlic in butter and oil until onion is transparent. Add broth, potatoes, tomatoes, celery, herbs, salt and pepper, and simmer until the potatoes are just soft. Then add fish meat and parsley and reheat. Serves 3-4.

Waitemata Welsh Rarebit
2 tbsp butter
½ tsp salt
¼ tsp dry mustard
350g tasty cheddar cheese, grated
1 cup beer
1 egg, beaten
hamburger buns or bread rolls
paprika
parsley, chopped

Melt butter in a saucepan and add seasonings and cheese. Gently heat until cheese is melted, stirring constantly. Mix in beer and just before serving mix in the egg. Halve the buns or rolls and toast and butter them. Pour the saucepan mixture over buns and sprinkle with paprika and parsley. Serves 4.

Penny's Pasta
450g spaghetti, egg noodles or macaroni
1 onion, diced
2 tbsp oil
2 cloves garlic, minced
2 tbsp capers
3 tomatoes, chopped
1 cup green peas
1 tbsp dried parsley
1 tsp mixed herbs

Cook pasta until just soft and drain off water. Sauté onion in oil until transparent. Add garlic and cook until the onion turns golden. Add capers, tomatoes, peas and parsley. Cook mixture 10-15 minutes over a medium heat. Add mixed herbs, toss with pasta and serve. Serves 6.

Lamb Oriental
1 cup of lamb cut into 25mm cubes
2 tbsp sherry
1 tbsp soy sauce
½ tsp salt
2 onions, chopped
2 tbsp oil
½ cup sliced bamboo shoots

Marinate meat in sherry, soy sauce and salt. Brown onions in oil in a frying pan or wok and add meat (after draining off marinade) and bamboo shoots. Stir-fry on high heat for 3 minutes and serve immediately with rice. Serves 4.

Twisty Pasta

1 cup courgettes, sliced
450g twisty pasta noodles
½ cup parmesan cheese, grated
½ cup red or green peppers, sliced

Steam courgettes until tender. Boil pasta until tender and drain. While still hot, mix courgettes, cheese and pepper into the pasta and toss. Serves 6.

Port Fitzroy Paella

1 chicken, cut into pieces
2 onions, chopped
1 stalk celery, finely chopped
2 carrots, diced
2 tsp salt
black pepper
¼ cup oil
2 cups rice
2 cloves garlic, minced
1 cup peas
½ tsp oregano
pinch of saffron or turmeric
1 can shrimps
1 can mussels or 12 fresh mussels

To 6 cups of water in a saucepan add chicken, onions, celery, carrots, and salt and pepper. Bring to the boil, then cover and simmer for 1 hour. Strain and reserve 4 cups of broth. Bone the chicken and dice the meat. Heat oil in a frypan and fry rice and garlic, stirring constantly until rice is browned. Add remainder of ingredients, except shrimps and mussels, cover and cook over a low heat for 10-15 minutes. Add shrimps and mussels. Cover and heat for 5 minutes more. Serves 6.

Rangitoto Ratatouille

1 onion, minced
¼ cup oil
1 clove garlic, minced
1½ tbsp flour
1 courgette, sliced
1 eggplant, cubed
1 green pepper, cut into strips
2 tomatoes, peeled and sliced
salt and pepper to taste
½ tsp capers

Sauté onion and garlic in oil until onion is transparent. Flour courgette and eggplant pieces lightly and add with peppers to frypan. Cook slowly for 1 hour. Add tomatoes and simmer uncovered until mixture thickens. Season. Add capers and cook for a further 10 minutes. Serve hot or cold. Serves 4.

Tartare Sauce

$^{1/2}$ cup mayonnaise
1 tsp prepared mustard
dash lemon juice
1 onion, minced
1 gherkin, finely chopped
salt to taste
Combine all ingredients.

Tuna Lunch

450g shell macaroni
1 tin tuna
lemon juice to taste
hard-boiled eggs
2 tbsp mayonnaise
pinch dill seed
Cook macaroni until just tender and drain. Add all other ingredients, toss and leave to cool. Serves 5.

Mollie's Drop Scones

2 cups plain flour
3 tsp baking powder
pinch of salt
1 tbsp melted butter
2 tbsp sugar
1 egg
$^{1/2}$-1 cup milk
Combine ingredients and mix well together. Heat oil in frypan and drop spoonfuls of mixture into it. Reduce heat as mixture cooks quickly. When bubbles form in the surface of scones, turn over and cook onother side for a little while longer. Excellent with canned cream and jam.

Potato Fritters
2 Cups mashed potato
1 egg
1 tbsp flour
salt and pepper
1 tsp fresh or dried parsley
breadcrumbs or flour

Combine first five ingredients and mix well together. Form into medium-sized flat cakes and roll in breadcrumbs (or flour). Cook in frypan in a little butter or oil for 2 minutes each side.

Hedgehogs
1 kg mince
2 onions, chopped
2 rashers bacon
1 cup rice
parsley
1 can tomato juice
pepper and salt to taste

Combine ingredients and roll into balls. Cook in pressure cooker for 20-30 minutes. Serve hot or cold.

Dortés
Sour dough bread for extended cruising is easy. Make up a flour and water 'bug' in a jar, feed it 1 tablespoon of plain flour a day and keep it to yoghurt consistency.
To make bread:
    1 cup plain flour mixed with 'bug'
    2 cups plain flour
    2 cups rye flour
    2 tsp sea salt
    1 tbsp sugar
    fresh water

Divide the flour with bug into two. Use half and retain half for use later. Mix the half you are using with all other ingredients. Spray bread pans with non-stick oil. Rise bread in pans. Bake about 1 hour at around 180°C, depending on your stove. Bread that sounds hollow when tapped is cooked.

glossary

A

Aback: describes a sail that the wind has struck on its lee side.

Abeam: at right angles to the boat's midships.

Aft: at or near the stern.

Anti-fouling: a paint compound used to prevent marine growths on the underwater area of the hull.

Apparent wind: a combination of true wind and that created by the movement of the boat.

Astern: behind the boat; to go astern is to steer the boat in reverse.

Athwartships: at right angles to the boat's fore-and-aft line.

B

Back a sail: to force it against the wind, sheeting it to windward. Used when manoeuvring to make the boat fall off the wind.

Backstay: a stay that supports the mast from at or near the stern and prevents forward movement of the mast.

Ballast: heavy weight, usually iron or lead, which is placed low in the boat to provide stability.

Ballast keel: ballast bolted to the keel to increase the boat's stability and prevent it from capsizing.

Batten: a light, flexible strip of wood or plastic inserted into a batten pocket in the leech of the sail to give the sail shape and support.

Beam: the widest part of a boat; 'on the beam' is the same as 'abeam'.

Bear away: to steer away from the wind.

Bearing: the compass direction of an object from an observer.

Beat: to sail close-hauled on a zigzag course towards the wind, on alternate tacks.

Belay: to secure a rope around a cleat.

Berth: a sleeping place on board a boat; to moor a boat; a boat's moored position in a harbour or marina.

Bilge: the lower inside area of the hull against the outside edge.

Block: a pulley in a wooden or plastic case, consisting of a sheave (a grooved wheel) around which a rope runs.

Boom preventer: prevents boom gybing and the boat rolling.

Boot-topping: a narrow stripe painted around the hull above the waterline and which separates the bottom paint from the topside finish.

Broach: to slew broadside to the wind and heel when running before the wind, usually resulting in loss of control.

Broad reach: with the wind aft, any point of sailing between a beam reach and running.

Bulkhead: partition wall in the hull of the boat usually fitted athwartships.

C

Catamaran: a sailing boat with twin hulls.

Centreboard: a board or metal plate lowered through a slot in the keelson or hull to reduce leeway.

Centre-line: the centre of a boat in a fore-and aft line.

Chainplate: a metal plate bolted to the side of the boat or bulkhead, to which the rigging is connected.

Chart datum: a reference level on a chart below which the tide does not usually fall. Seabed soundings are given below chart datum.

Chine: the line on a hull where the bilge meets the topsides.

Claw ring: a fitting used on the boom after roller reefing the mainsail. It slips over the boom like a claw and to it is attached the main sheet or boom vang.

Cleat: a horned fitting around which a rope is belayed, or secured.

Clevis pin: a locking pin through which a split ring is inserted to prevent the ring's accidental removal.

Clew: the after, lower corner of a sail at the junction of the foot and leech.

Close-hauled: the point of sailing closest to the wind.

Close reach: the point of sailing between closehauled and a beam reach.

Close-winded: a boat's ability to sail very close to the wind.

Coamings: the raised structure round the cockpit and hatch, which stops water entering. The sides of the cabin top are also coamings.

Course: the direction in which a vessel is steered.

Cringle: an eye, often with a metal lining, worked into the sail.

D

Dead run: running with the wind blowing straight aft.

Deviation: compass error caused by magnetic attraction of metal objects on the boat. It is the difference, measured in degrees, between the magnetic course and direction indicated by the compass.

Displacement: the weight of sea-water displaced by the submerged part of the boat and which is exactly equal to the boat's weight.
Downhaul: a rope fitted to pull down a sail or boom.
Draft: the depth of water a boat requires in order to float, being the vertical distance from the waterline to the bottom of the keel.
Drop keel: a retractable keel, which can be drawn into the hull.

E
Eye of the wind: the direction from which the true wind blows.

F
Fairlead: a fitting used to guide a rope, wire or chain to alter its direction.
Fathom: the unit of depth measurement: 1 fathom = 6ft = 1.83m.
Fid: a tapered wooden tool used in splicing rope and for sailmaking.
Fix: the accurate positioning of a boat found by the intersection of two or more bearing lines.
Forestay: the foremost stay, running from the masthead forward to the stem.
Freeboard: height of the side of the boat from the waterline to the deck.

G
Genoa: a large headsail, which overlaps the mast; it is hoisted in light winds.
Gimbals: a device consisting of two rings pivoted to provide a base that stays level despite a boat's motion; used for compass, lights, cooker.
Go about: to turn the boat through the eye of the wind to change tack.

Gooseneck: the fitting that attaches the boom to the mast.
Goosewing: to have the headsail poled out to windward on a run, so that headsail and mainsail are out to opposite sides of the boat, like wings.
Ground tackle: general term used for anchoring gear, including anchor, cable, warp, etc.
Gudgeon: a rudder fitting. A metal eye set into the transom or rudder into which the pintle fits.
Guy: a rope controlling a spar; a spinnaker guy controls the fore-and-aft position of the spinnaker pole; the fore guy controls the movement of the outer end of the pole.
Gybe: to change tack by turning the stern through the wind; by turning the bow of the boat towards the main boom.

H
Halyard: rope or wire used to hoist and lower sails.
Hank: fitting used to attach the luff of a headsail to a stay.
Hatch: an opening in the deck giving access to the interior.
Head-to-wind: with the bow headed right into the eye of the wind.
Headfoil: a streamlined forestay surround, which has a groove into which the headsail luff slides.
Head: the toilet.
Headway: the forward movement of a boat through the water.
Heave-to: to back the jib so the boat slows nearly to a stop. The tiller is held to leeward at the same time.
Heel: the leaning over of the boat due to pressure of the

wind on the sails.

I
In irons: describes a boat stalled head-to-wind, while tacking and unable to bear off one way or the other. In order to get under way again, all sails should be sheeted in and the helm held hard over on one side.

J
Jibe: see Gybe
Jury rig: a temporary rig to replace lost or damaged gear.

K
Kedge: a small, light second anchor.
Keel: the main backbone of the boat running fore and aft and supporting the frame. In a keel yacht, the ballast keel is bolted to this main beam, or a centreboard passes through it in the case of unballasted yachts.
Ketch: a two-masted sailing vessel, the smaller, aft, mizzen mast stepped forward of the rudder post.
Kicking trap: a line used to pull the boom down and keep tension on the mainsail. Used particularly on a reach or run.

L
Lanyard: a short line attached to one object to secure it to another, for example a harness lanyard.
Leech: the after edge of a sail from head to clew.
Lee helm: the tendency of a boat to bear off the wind, the helm needing to be kept to leeward to hold course.
Lee shore: a shore which the wind is blowing to.
Leeward: away from the wind; the direction to which the wind is going (opposite of windward).

Leeway: the sideways drift of a boat off its course to leeward.

Let fly: to let a sheet go instantly, spilling the wind from the sails.

Lifelines: wires or ropes strung around a boat on stanchions to prevent the crew falling overboard.

List: a boat's more or less permanent lean to one side, owing to shifting ballast and/or accumulation of water.

Log: an instrument for determining a boat's speed and distance travelled through the water; to record the details of a voyage.

Luff: the forward edge of a sail. To luff up is to bring the boat's head into the wind.

M

Marlin spike: a pointed steel or wooden spike used to separate the strands of rope when splicing.

Mast step: the through-deck channel, leading to an attachment in the keel, into which the mast is placed.

Member: a structural timber, part of the skeleton of the hull.

Meridian: an imaginary line around the earth, which passes through the poles and intersects the equator at right angles. All lines of longitude are meridians.

Mizzen: the aftermost mast on a ketch or yawl; a sail set on the mizzen mast.

O

Off the wind: sailing downwind.

On the wind: close-hauled.

Outhaul: a rope used for hauling out the foot of a sail.

Overall length (LOA): the boat's extreme length, measured from the foremost part of the

bow to the aftermost part of the stern.

P

Painter: the rope attached to the bows of a dinghy or tender, by which it is towed or made fast.

Pintle: an upright pin attached to a boat's transom or rudder and which slips into the gudgeon to form a hinged pivot.

Pitch: the fore-and-aft rocking of a boat.

Points of sailing: the different angles to the wind on which a boat may sail; the boat's course relative to the direction of the wind.

Port: the left side of a boat looking forward (opposite of starboard).

Port tack: when the wind comes from the port side and the mainsail is out to starboard.

Position line: a line drawn on a chart from a bearing and along which the boat's position lies. Two or more position lines give a fix.

Pulpit: a metal guard-rail at the bows of a boat, which provides safety for crew working forward, changing headsails, etc.

Pushpit: a metal guard-rail fitted at the stern.

Q

Quarter: the side of the boat aft of the beam.

R

Rake: the fore-and-aft inclination of a mast or other feature of a boat from the perpendicular.

Reach: to sail with the wind roughly on the beam; any point of sailing between running and close-hauled.

Reef: to reduce the sail area

by taking it in at the foot and folding or rolling surplus material on the boom.

Reefing line: strong line with which the leech cringle is pulled down to the boom when reefing.

Rigging screw: a fitting with which the tension of standing rigging is adjusted.

Roach: the curved part of the leech of a sail extending beyond the direct line from head to clew.

Run: to sail directly downwind with the sheets eased well out.

Running rigging: all of the moving lines such as sheets, halyards, guys used in the support and control of sails and spars.

S

Schooner: a boat with two or more masts with the mainmast aft.

Scuppers: an opening in the toe rail that allows water to drain off the deck or cockpit.

Seacock: a shut-off valve on underwater inlet or outlet piping through the hull.

Sea room: room in which a boat can manoeuvre without danger of collision or grounding.

Shackle: a metal link of varying shape with a removable bolt across the open end, used to secure lines to sails, poles, etc.

Sheave: a grooved wheel in a block or spar upon which a rope runs.

Sheet: a rope controlling a sail.

Shrouds: ropes or wires, usually in pairs, reaching from the mast to the chain plates at the sides of the boat to prevent the mast falling sideways.

Skin fitting: a through-hull

fitting through which air or water passes. A seacock is fitted to close the hole when not in use.

Sloop: a single-masted boat with a mainsail and one headsail.

Spar: a general term for masts, booms, poles.

Spinnaker: a large, light, balloon-shaped sail set in front of the bows when the wind is aft of the beam.

Splice: to join two ropes or wires or make an eye splice in the end of a line by unlaying their strands and interweaving them.

Spreaders: horizontal struts attached to the mast, which spread the shrouds out from the mast and improve their support of the mast.

Stall: a sail stalls when the airflow over it stops.

Stanchion: upright metal post bolted to the deck to support guard rails or lifelines.

Standing part: the part of a rope that is secured to an object, opposite to the hauling part.

Standing rigging: the shrouds and stays that are permanently set up and support the mast.

Starboard: the right side of a boat looking forward (opposite of port).

Starboard tack: when the wind comes from the starboard side and the mainsail is out to port.

Stay: a wire or rope that supports the mast in a fore-and-aft direction; part of the standing rigging.

Steerage way: having sufficient speed for the boat to be steered, or to answer the helm.

Stem: the timber at the bow, reaching from the forward end of the keel, to which the two sides of the boat are attached.

Stringer: a fore-and-aft structural timber fitted to strengthen the frames.

Strop: a loop of wire or rope used to raise the tack of a headsail some distance off the deck.

Strop down: to secure a rope or wire so that it does not fly about and become entangled.

T

Tack: to turn the boat through the wind – either by gybing or going about – so that it blows on the opposite side of the sails; also the lower forward corner of a sail.

Tacking: working to windward or downwind by sailing close-hauled on alternate courses so that the wind is first on one side of the boat, then on the other.

Tackle: a purchase system consisting of rope and blocks and which is used to gain mechanical advantage.

Tang: a metal fitting on a mast or other spar to which standing rigging is attached.

Toe rail: the raised edge of the deck where it meets the hull.

Topping lift: rope or wire used to adjust boom height.

Topsides: the sides of a boat between the waterline and the deck.

Track: the course a boat has made; a fitting on the mast or boom into which the slides on a sail fit; also, a deck fitting along which a traveller runs.

Traveller: a fitting that slides in a track and is used to alter the angle of the sheets.

Trim: to adjust the angle of the sails, by means of sheets, so that they are at their best shape and angle to the wind.

Turnbuckle: see Rigging screw.

V

Veer: the wind veers when it changes direction clockwise.

W

Wake: the disturbed water left behind a boat.

Waterline: the horizontal line along the hull, at which a boat floats.

Waterline length (WL): the length of a boat from stem to stern at the waterline.

Weather helm: the tendency for a boat to come up into the wind (opposite of lee helm).

Weather side: the side of a boat on which the wind is blowing.

Wetted surface: the area of the hull under water.

Whisker pole: a light pole used on a small yacht to hold out the headsail when running.

Windlass: a winch used to haul up the anchor chain.

Windward: the direction from which the wind blows; towards the wind (opposite of leeward).

Y

Yaw: erratic movement of a boat off its course.

Yawl: a two-masted boat with the smaller mizzen mast stepped aft of the rudder post.

index

Note: numbers in bold italic indicate pages in the colour section

about the author

Penny Whiting was born in 1949 and is the youngest of a family of five children.

Her passion for the sea has been encouraged all her life. At age 2 she began her sailing adventures in a two-man yacht with her father D'Arcy. She owned her own yacht at age 9 and, from age 16, sailed with her father and her brother in Whangarei to Noumea ocean races on the family's 36-foot yacht, *Coruba*.

She barely missed representing New Zealand at the Jamaica Games as a competitive swimmer, but went on to represent her country as a surfer at the World Championships held in Puerto Rico in 1968.

Penny has two grown-up children, Carl and Erin. Carl sails for Team NZ and Erin is an in-house fitter for a fashion company. She also participates in competitive horse riding events.

Penny was an Auckland City Councillor for six years, serving three years on her local community board before being elected. She was also Chairman for the Auckland Zoo for six years, a time that gave her fantastic insight into the lives of exotic animals.

Penny's sailing school has been operating for over 30 years. She describes herself as a 'one-man band', tending to the teaching, administration tasks and the maintenance of her yacht herself.

Her 50-foot yacht, *Endless Summer*, was designed by her brother and built by the family at Onehunga. Penny spends many hours aboard, either solo sailing or teaching classes. Over the years she has owned three 50-foot yachts. In her early teaching days she would often 'steal' her father's yacht to use for her sailing school.

In 1994 Penny was awarded an MBE by the Queen for her services to sailing. She is a keen tennis player, artist and potter but points out she still hangs out the laundry and tries to keep up with her kids!

Penny has published three books including her biography, *Endless Summer*, which was released in 2000. She has also released a learn to sail video which was filmed aboard *Endless Summer*. Penny lives in Auckland and says 'Sailing is my life'.